SCHOLASTIC

Teaching Writing Through Differentiated Instruction With Leveled Graphic Organizers

Nancy L. Witherell and Mary C. McMackin

NEW YORK · TORONTO · LONDON · AUCKLAND · SYDNEY
MEXICO CITY · NEW DELHI · HONG KONG · BUENOS AIRES

Teaching *Resources*

Dedication

■ ■ ■ ■ ■ ■ ■ ■ ■ ■ ■ ■

To my sister, Genie Stonesifer, and my brothers Anthony Kopcych, Jr., Robert Kopcych, Peter Kopcych, and especially to my brother Howard Kopcych, a noneducator who ran out and bought three copies of our first book, with love.—NLW

To my brothers, sister-in-law, and nieces (the Carew family): Bob, John, Anita, Jennifer, Meghan, Danielle, and Colleen, with love.—MCM

We would like to send a special thank you to our editor, Sarah Longhi of Scholastic Teaching Resources, for all her help and guidance throughout this process. And of course, our greatest thanks go to the main support team, our husbands and children.

Cover design by Maria Lilja

Interior design by Sydney Wright

ISBN: 0-439-56727-0

Copyright © 2005 by Nancy L. Witherell and Mary C. McMackin.

Published by Scholastic Inc.

Printed in the U.S.A.

3 4 5 6 7 8 9 10   40   14 13 12 11 10 09 08 07

Contents

Introduction

"You've got to read this!" boasts a teacher who just read an incredible piece of writing by one of her students. Her voice rings with delight and pride. Teachers feel such joy when sharing wonderful stories, reports, or poems that their students have written. Both teacher and student have worked hard to get to this point and have earned the right to celebrate.

Guiding children to write well and produce excellent writing samples takes dedication, persistence, and time to practice, yet it can be extremely rewarding. It is our hope that this book will help you in your pursuit of growing wonderful writers. The explanations and graphic organizers in this text are meant to help make your teaching more powerful and your planning easier.

What Are Tiered Graphic Organizers?

Tiered graphic organizers are leveled, visual planners on which students record information in a logical way. The recorded information is then used in the writing activity. According to Tomlinson (1999), teachers can modify *content*, *process*, or *product* to meet the diverse needs of learners. When using tiered graphic organizers, teachers are modifying the product. Bender (2002)

acknowledges that it is through the product that "learning is observed and evaluated." Students demonstrate what they know and can do through the products they create. If the task is too easy or too difficult, it doesn't reflect the student's full potential. You'll see that organizers on three instructional levels (introductory, intermediate, and challenging) accompany each skill introduced in this book. By designing graphic organizers at three different levels, we offer teachers the necessary materials to match students with "just right" activities.

Why Use Tiered Graphic Organizers?

In order to meet the diverse needs of students in today's classroom, teachers must be able to design lessons that (1) meet individual instructional requirements, (2) stay within what is often mandated curriculum, and (3) ensure consistent outcomes for all students. Time constraints place limits on the amount of individual instruction we can provide. In *Teaching Writing Through Differentiated Instruction With Leveled Graphic Organizers*, we've structured each whole-class mini-lesson around one central objective and then modified the follow-up activities to meet student

needs. For example, our objective for descriptive writing is "to write a clear description of an object." We've included in the chapter specific directions for instruction. Adjectives, sensory images, and similes are introduced. All students participate in the lesson. Not all students will be successful, however, if given the same follow-up, reinforcing activity to complete. That's where the tiered graphic organizers come in. Students are not responsible for learning at the same pace, yet each one is responsible for demonstrating an understanding at a level that is developmentally appropriate.

How Is This Book Organized?

Each chapter focuses on a specific writing skill and includes:

* a description of the target skill and criteria to use in measuring understanding of the skill

* a model passage that illustrates the target skill

* a mini-lesson, which can be used for whole-class, initial instruction

* instructional tips

* suggested texts (mostly children's literature) where additional examples of the skill can be found

* three tiered graphic organizers for students to use to demonstrate their understanding of the skill.

The chapters in the book are designed as both stand-alone chapters and as units of study that reinforce and extend learning across several chapters. For example, if you are working on persuasive writing, you may want to include in your instructional plans the chapter on persuasive writing. When completed, it may make sense to introduce the chapter on book reports, where students apply what they've learned about persuasion to make recommendations for or against the books they review.

Is This a Workbook?

No. We struggled with our philosophical stance as we created this book. It is not, and has never been, our intent to write a workbook for writing. Although workbooks may be appropriate to use with some students in some situations, they often focus on subsets of skills and tasks that are closed (as opposed to open-ended), such as circling all the adverbs in a series of sentences. Generally, too, workbook pages are used one time; once the answers have been identified, the page has served its purpose. Conversely, the activities in this book are open-ended and may be used over and over again as your students continue to grow and develop. They are designed to help students build awareness of criteria that distinguish one form of writing from another. For example, we investigate what it takes to write an effective memoir (page 79), to create dialogue that moves a plot along

(page 73), to write figurative language that makes writing more interesting (page 19), and so on. As teachers, we need to analyze writing products, deduce the criteria, and be assured that our students understand the components and expectations of the writing task at hand. This book does not address isolated skills; rather, it examines the content, processes, and differentiated products that move students from being less experienced to more accomplished writers.

How Should I Use the Graphic Organizers?

We designed the graphic organizers to be used with a wide variety of topics and experiences. Teachers tend to use them in two ways: first, to differentiate instruction and products in order to meet the needs of individual learners, as discussed, and second, as a scaffolding experience. As such, a student may be matched to a graphic organizer at the introductory level and be successful. Then, along with additional instruction and teacher support, the student can work through the levels in sequence to develop the skills necessary to complete the more cognitively challenging activities.

It is our intention to have the graphic organizers in each chapter look equally as appealing and demanding. We don't want a student working at the introductory level to think her work is less rigorous than that of a student working at a higher level, and vice versa. If matched carefully, all students should be working at a "just right" level. You may want to enlarge the graphic organizers to 11 by 14 inches when students work in pairs or need more space than is provided.

Final Thoughts

It is our hope that this book will inspire you to design other focused lessons and tiered graphic organizers to supplement your writing instruction and address the needs of your students. We are confident that the tiered organizers, paired with focused instruction, will help students improve the quality of their writing.

Professional Works Cited

Bender, W. N. (2002). *Differentiating instruction for students with learning disabilities: Best teaching practices for general and special educators.* Thousand Oaks, CA: Corwin Press.

Kaufer, D. S., & Carley, K. (1994). Some concepts and axioms about communication: Proximate and at a distance. *Written communication, 11* (1), 8–42.

Tomlinson, C. A. (1999). *The differentiated classroom: Responding to the needs of all learners.* Alexandria, VA: ASCD.

Writing Paragraphs

Skill: *Organize a series of related sentences around one topic.*

Overview

A paragraph is a well-organized set of sentences that focuses on one "controlling," or main, idea. A paragraph has a beginning (topic sentence), a middle (body), and an end (a closing or transition to the next paragraph). The topic sentence states what the paragraph will be about, while the sentences that follow it provide details, examples, and descriptions that explain the main idea. The final sentence is used to bring closure if the paragraph is standing alone. If the paragraph is going to lead to another one, the writer will need to make a smooth transition to the next paragraph.

Model

> Camping is not for me. Last summer I went on a dreaded camping trip with my parents, my sister Katie, Aunt Anita, Uncle John, and my four cousins, Colleen, Danielle, Meghan, and Jennifer. I was the only boy. By the time we got to the campsite and struggled to set up the tents, I was eaten alive by bugs. While I scratched, Mom sprayed insect repellent, which gagged me. She continued to spray it even though it was landing on the food that was being prepared for our first campsite dinner. The food was nothing to write home about. I managed to get a burger that was burnt on the outside and raw on the inside. Mom told me not to worry. This is the same person who told me that I couldn't bring my computer or cell phone. I had no connection with the outside world. This was particularly scary as nightfall approached. It would have been nice to have a phone because I knew there were wild animals not far away. That's why I slept with one eye open the entire first night. The second day was pretty much a repeat of the first. By the second night, I was counting down the days until my return to civilization—video games, fast food, the mall, TV remote, and my own soft bed.

How to Teach

Begin by writing the model paragraph on chart paper or copying it onto a transparency. Spend a few minutes examining this model with students. On a piece of chart paper, make a chart like the one on page 8, putting the main idea at the

top (*Why I don't like camping*) and having students help you list the details that support this main idea in the left column (*bugs, food, no computer, no cell phone, wild animals*). Be sure students understand that the details you listed are in this order to show the events of the writer's day in sequence. In the right column, list how the writer elaborated each detail. Explain that you'll take notes in the right column; you won't use complete sentences.

Why I don't like camping...

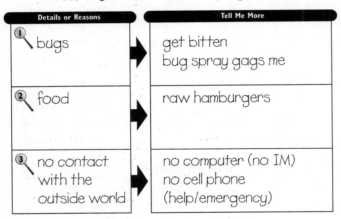

Details or Reasons	Tell Me More
① bugs	get bitten bug spray gags me
② food	raw hamburgers
③ no contact with the outside world	no computer (no IM) no cell phone (help/emergency)

How to Teach

Next, show students a blank two-column chart. Ask them to suggest topic ideas for a different paragraph, or provide a topic sentence such as "We love to play games outdoors." Together, brainstorm details (list them in the left column) and then examples or descriptions they can use to explain each detail (list them in the right column). Before beginning to write, reread the list of details and talk about how to arrange them. Is there one idea that should go first? Do some ideas fit together? Would it be best to leave a particular one for the

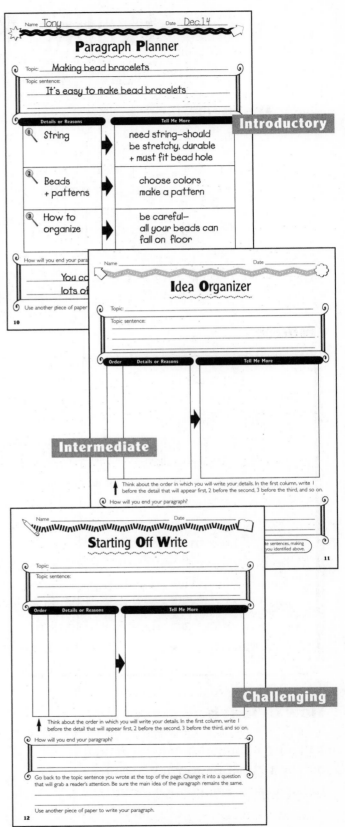

end? Invite a volunteer to number the notes in the left column, illustrating a well-thought-out arrangement of ideas. It's much easier to number the ideas before writing than to make major revisions after a draft is written.

Now you're ready to write. With students' help, refer back to the chart and discuss how to phrase each sentence, making sure to include enough detail to support the main idea. Act as scribe as students offer suggestions. As each idea is used, check it off the chart. This helps to keep everyone organized.

Literature Sources for Other Models

Lasky, K. (1981). *The night journey.* New York: Frederick Warne. (See p. 2, para. 4.)

Smith, R. K. (1987). *Mostly Michael.* New York: Dell Yearling Books (See p. 8, para. 1.)

Facklam, M. (2003). *Lizards weird and wonderful.* New York: Little, Brown and Company. (See "Glass Snakes.")

Teacher to Teacher

Many students find it difficult to write effective paragraphs because they haven't developed their details or organized their ideas logically. Yet, the problem with asking students to "tell more," without modeling the process of writing a paragraph, is that they may simply list additional ideas rather than write a richer explanation. For

example, "tell me more" about "We love to play games outdoors" could become "At recess we play dodge ball, tag, and basketball." It's fine to include the names of games, but we need to model how to dig deeper, how to extrapolate something more significant, how to get students to connect back to the main idea (why I like outdoor recess) and provide support for it. We might say, "I'm glad you play so many games. Tell me what it is about these games that you like so much."

Using the Tiered Organizers

When your students can organize thoughts around a main idea, they are ready to use one of the following graphic organizers.

Introductory: **Paragraph Planner**
Students write a topic sentence, provide three details for it, and support each detail with relevant information. They also write a concluding sentence.

Intermediate: **Idea Organizer**
Students write a topic sentence, provide four details for it, and support each detail with relevant information. They also write a concluding sentence. Before beginning their first draft, they arrange the details in a logical order.

Challenging: **Starting Off Write**
Students first complete the same activities as those for the intermediate level, then they revise the topic sentence, changing it into an open-ended question.

Name _____   Date _____

Paragraph Planner

Topic: _____

Topic sentence: _____

_____

_____

Details or Reasons	Tell Me More
①	
②	
③	

How will you end your paragraph?

_____

_____

Use another piece of paper to write your paragraph.

Change your notes into complete sentences.

Idea Organizer

Topic: _____

Topic sentence:

_____

_____

_____

Order	Details or Reasons	Tell Me More

Think about the order in which you will write your details. In the first column, write 1 before the detail that will appear first, 2 before the second, 3 before the third, and so on.

How will you end your paragraph?

_____

_____

Use another piece of paper to write your paragraph.

Change your notes into complete sentences, making sure your ideas are in the order you identified above.

Starting Off Write

Topic: _____

Topic sentence: _____

_____

_____

Order	Details or Reasons	Tell Me More

↑ Think about the order in which you will write your details. In the first column, write 1 before the detail that will appear first, 2 before the second, 3 before the third, and so on.

How will you end your paragraph?

_____

_____

Go back to the topic sentence you wrote at the top of the page. Change it into a question that will grab a reader's attention. Be sure the main idea of the paragraph remains the same.

_____

_____

Use another piece of paper to write your paragraph.

Finding a Voice

Skill: *Use language that conveys one's personality.*

Overview

For many of us, "voice" is a nebulous element of writing. We all talk about adding voice, but what exactly do we mean? It's difficult to define *voice* because it is a stylistic quality unique to each writer and to each purpose. By *voice* we're really talking about the result created from the use of words—a product, not a process. Voice is the result of word choice, sentence length, images, and details presented. All these pieces come together to reveal a personality behind the words, the unique characteristics, attitudes, and feelings of the writer.

Model

Finding Love

It's been almost fourteen years since my sister, my parents, and I stood in the basement of Mrs. Lake's house watching a litter of English Springer Spaniels run wildly around, jumping on us, barking at each other, and investigating every available nook and cranny. They had no way of knowing that they were auditioning for an important part in our future.

Some puppies were black and white, others brown (or, as I was informed, liver) and white. Each one had an adorable face, with big eyes and long floppy ears. If given the chance, I would have picked George, a peppy black and white male who got this name because he was so curious. But I knew the puppy was going to be Mom's birthday present. She would choose.

To my delight, George came home with us. Mom wanted him to have an English name, so we called him Thatcher, after Margaret, the prime minister of England. Thatch, as he came to be called, quickly learned to shake, fetch, and give kisses. I even taught him how to retrieve the mail sticking through the slot in the front door. He had to stop doing this, though, when Mom complained that the bills had holes from Thatcher's teeth.

Today Thatcher doesn't race around the yard like he once did. The arthritis in his back legs has slowed him down. Even making his way up and down the steps is difficult. When he loses his footing and falls, which seems to happen quite regularly now, he looks up with his sad, hopeful eyes for someone to boost him upright again. He's glad to have a friend help him and quickly returns the favor with a shake, kiss, or wag of his stubby tail. For the last few years, Thatch has shared our house with a younger Springer, Tessa, a brown (or, should I say, liver) female. She's nice, I guess, but she sure isn't any Thatcher!

How to Teach

Let's take a closer look at the model above. Ask, *What words, details, and images were used to express the strong feelings the author has for Thatcher?* Record the ideas on a chart like the following:

<u>Words:</u> adorable; curious; sad, hopeful eyes.

<u>Phrases:</u> "To my delight," "She's nice, I guess, but she sure isn't any Thatcher."

<u>Details:</u> dog used to race around but doesn't now, has arthritis, falls easily

<u>Images:</u> puppies playing; Thatcher learning to shake, give kisses, retrieve mail; Thatch is helped up and he shakes, kisses, or wags stubby tail.

Next, talk about how these words create feelings of love and sadness. While reading books with students, select passages in which the author's or character's voice shines through. In pairs, ask students to determine if it's the word choice, sentence construction, details, images, or some other factor that conveys feelings, attitudes, emotions, or a particular stand on an issue.

To reinforce this idea, you may create "voiceless" passages and have students work together to revise the passages so a voice is evident. Here's one to use:

> I went to the beach with my family. We made sand castles. A wave knocked over my sand castle. Later we played in the arcade. After dinner, we went home.

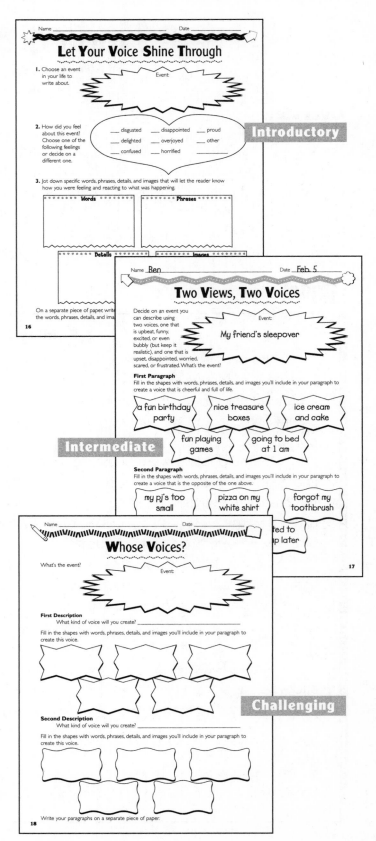

14

Work together and have students experiment as they revise. What happens if you add long, complex sentences or short, choppy phrases? If you make the language more formal or colloquial? If you change the details, delete some, or add others? If you insert dialogue? Encourage students to make a conscious effort to create a personality and attitude that their readers can recognize. Once students begin to write with voice, have them share their work as models for others.

Literature Sources for Other Models

Bonners, S. (2002). *Making music.* New York: Farrar, Straus & Giroux. (Read Mrs. Bergstrom in "New Neighbors.")

Lowry, L. (2002). *Gooney bird greene.* Boston: Houghton Mifflin Company. (See Ch. 2.)

Turner, A. (1987). *Nettie's trip south.* New York: Macmillan. (picture book)

Teacher to Teacher

It seems that younger writers have less difficulty writing with voice than do students in the upper elementary grades and beyond. Perhaps older students are reluctant to expose emotions, passions, or beliefs. In some cases, we can help students find their voices by having them slow down the pace of their writing and add relevant details to it.

Using the Tiered Organizers

While you are modeling ways in which voice can be created, check to see which students' voices are already coming through. Once this begins to happen, you are ready to match them with one of the activities that follow:

Introductory: **Let Your Voice Shine Through**
Students identify an event, decide what feelings they want to reveal as they write about the event, and brainstorm specific words, phrases, details, and images that bring out their voice.

Intermediate: **Two Views, Two Voices**
Students select words and phrases to describe an event in a voice that is happy, upbeat, funny, or excited. Next, they select words and phrases to describe this same event in a voice that is upset, disappointed, worried, scared, or frustrated. Specific words, phrases, details, and images help them convey these voices.

Challenging: **Whose Voices?**
Students choose an event and describe it using two different voices. They may write in the voices of characters wildly different from themselves. Specific words, phrases, details, and images help them enact the voices they choose.

Let Your Voice Shine Through

1. Choose an event in your life to write about.

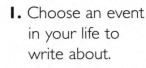 Event:

2. How did you feel about this event? Choose one of the following feelings or decide on a different one.

___ disgusted   ___ disappointed   ___ proud

___ delighted   ___ overjoyed   ___ other

___ confused   ___ horrified   _____

3. Jot down specific words, phrases, details, and images that will let the reader know how you were feeling and reacting to what was happening.

Words	Phrases

Details	Images

On a separate piece of paper, write a paragraph about this event. Make sure you include the words, phrases, details, and images that show what you were feeling and thinking.

Name _____ Date _____

Two Views, Two Voices

Decide on an event you can describe using two voices, one that is upbeat, funny, excited, or even bubbly (but keep it realistic), and one that is upset, disappointed, worried, scared, or frustrated. What's the event?

Event:

First Paragraph

Fill in the shapes with words, phrases, details, and images you'll include in your paragraph to create a voice that is cheerful and full of life.

Second Paragraph

Fill in the shapes with words, phrases, details, and images you'll include in your paragraph to create a voice that is the opposite of the one above.

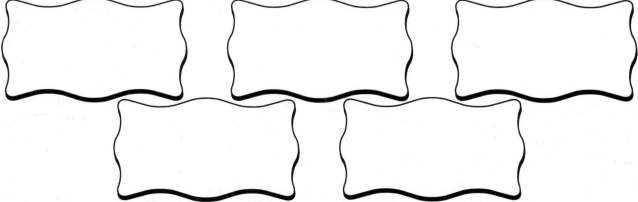

Write your paragraphs on a separate piece of paper.

Whose **V**oices?

What's the event?

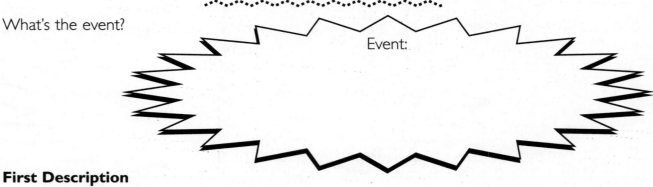

Event:

First Description

What kind of voice will you create? _____

Fill in the shapes with words, phrases, details, and images you'll include in your paragraph to create this voice.

Second Description

What kind of voice will you create? _____

Fill in the shapes with words, phrases, details, and images you'll include in your paragraph to create this voice.

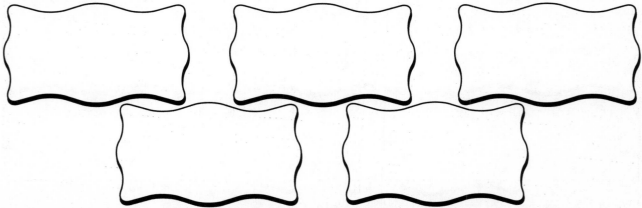

Write your paragraphs on a separate piece of paper.

Using Figurative Language

Skill: *Use hyperbole, metaphors, and similes to make writing more interesting.*

Overview

Metaphor, simile, and hyperbole are figures of speech that use comparison to make a point. In a metaphor, the comparison is implied, not directly stated, as in *Give him a shovel and he is a bulldozer* or *She is a songbird.* Similes compare two things that are not usually grouped together using the words *like* or *as*, such as *Your forehead is as hot as fire* or *His muscles are like steel.* Hyperbole is extravagant exaggeration in comparing one thing with another. Usually hyperbole is humorous—*It was so cold, I had icicles for hair* or *Tim ate at least a million pancakes!* In this chapter, we have chosen to focus on using hyperbole, although metaphor and simile can be taught in a similar manner. Hyperbole is a tool that writers with a well-developed sense of voice may choose to use. We recommend that you start with voice in the previous chapter prior to working on the creation of hyperboles.

Models

Boring	Vivid
Her room was a mess.	Her room was so messy it made a pigpen look clean.
The soup was bad.	The soup tasted like dandelions boiled in dirty water with pepper added to taste.
There were a lot of boats in the harbor.	It looked like the whole third fleet had weighed anchor in the harbor.
The meal was expensive.	I could have bought a new house for what that meal cost.

How to Teach

Conduct a mini-lesson on hyperbole in the context of writing, using tall tales, jokes, comical essays, stories, letters, or comic strips as examples. (Point out to students that similes and metaphors, on the other hand, are more likely to be found in narrative text and poetry.)

Explain hyperbole as a technique that helps writers make a point by describing something or an event in an overly dramatic way. Discuss the models above to show how hyperbole exaggerates without changing the meaning of the statement.

Now have students turn their own straightforward statements into hyperbole. To scaffold their writing, start by writing on the board a simple sentence, such as *The boy is very tall*, and then ask a volunteer to think up a funny exaggeration. Students enjoy out-doing one another; invite the class to brainstorm more exaggerations. Some replies might be:

> The boy is so tall, the Empire State Building looks short next to him.

> The boy is so tall, I felt like an ant when I looked up at him.

> That boy is as tall as Mount Everest.

As ideas are accepted, point out that the exaggeration does not change the meaning of the sentence. Students have just taken "very tall" and made it funny.

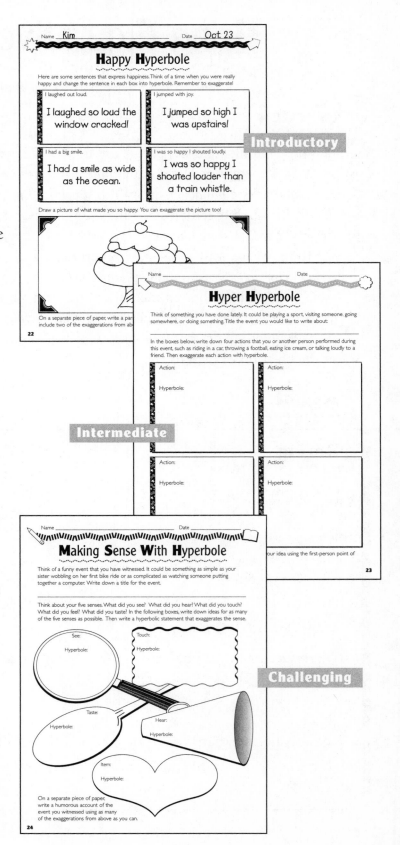

Once students are comfortable writing hyperbolic statements with the starter ideas, they are more apt to be successful independently. Have students think about something they did in the morning before school that could be exaggerated. (I brushed my teeth so white they looked like stars.)

Literature Sources for Other Models

Any tall tale makes a wonderful model. A few suggestions:

Schanzer, R. (2001). *David Crocket saves the world*. New York: HarperCollins.

Osborne, M. P., D. Carter & M. McCurdy (illustrator). (1991). *American tall tales*. New York: Alfred A. Knopf.

Isaacs, A. (1994). *Swamp angel*. New York: Puffin Books.

Teacher to Teacher

Students usually get the gist of hyperbolic statements, although sometimes they have problems coming up with extreme exaggerations of their own. For example, they may write, *The boy is as tall as a house*, rather than *The boy is as tall as Mount Everest*. The house comparison is not as comical, but it is still hyperbole and therefore acceptable. Some students may make statements that really do not exaggerate, such as, *The boy is as tall as his dad*. In this case we suggest the group brainstorm a number of extremely tall items. Students can then select and discuss the one or two ideas that give the reader the best picture.

Using the Tiered Organizers

When students are able to create acceptable hyperbole, choose one of the following graphic organizers.

Introductory: **Happy Hyperbole**
Students use starter ideas to write "happy hyperbole" and then a paragraph using two of their examples.

Intermediate: **Hyper Hyperbole**
Students think of actions and then write statements that exaggerate them. They use at least two of these hyperboles in a short first-person narrative.

Challenging: **Making Sense With Hyperbole**
Students generate exaggerations that depict the five senses and write humorous, hyperbolic accounts of an event using the exaggerations.

Happy Hyperbole

Here are some sentences that express happiness. Think of a time when you were really happy and change the sentence in each box into hyperbole. Remember to exaggerate!

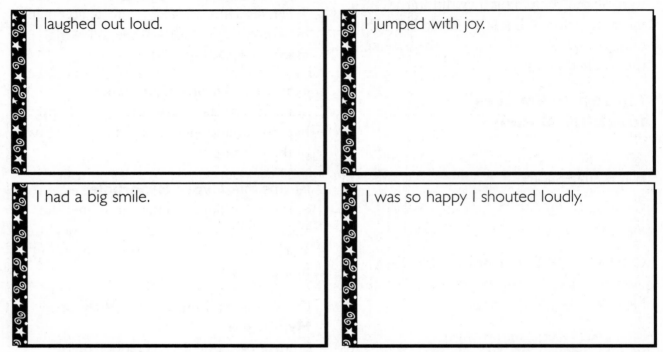

I laughed out loud.

I jumped with joy.

I had a big smile.

I was so happy I shouted loudly.

Draw a picture of what made you so happy. You can exaggerate the picture too!

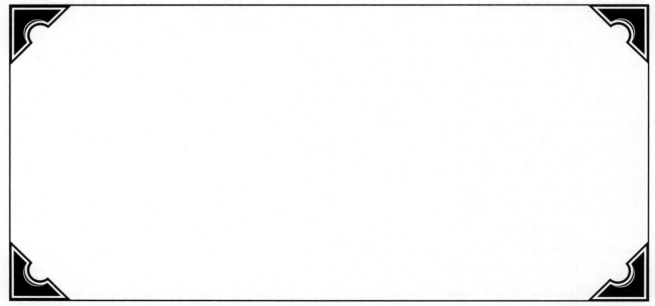

On a separate piece of paper, write a paragraph about the time you were so happy. Try to include two of the exaggerations from above.

Hyper Hyperbole

Think of something you have done lately. It could be playing a sport, visiting someone, going somewhere, or doing something. Title the event you would like to write about:

_____

In the boxes below, write down four actions that you or another person performed during this event, such as riding in a car, throwing a football, eating ice cream, or talking loudly to a friend. Then exaggerate each action with hyperbole.

Action:

Hyperbole:

Action:

Hyperbole:

Action:

Hyperbole:

Action:

Hyperbole:

On a separate piece of paper, write a story about your idea using the first-person point of view. Include at least two of the exaggerations.

Making Sense With Hyperbole

Think of a funny event that you have witnessed. It could be something as simple as your sister wobbling on her first bike ride or as complicated as watching someone putting together a computer. Write down a title for the event.

_____

Think about your five senses. What did you see? What did you hear? What did you touch? What did you feel? What did you taste? In the following boxes, write down ideas for as many of the five senses as possible. Then write a hyperbolic statement that exaggerates the sense.

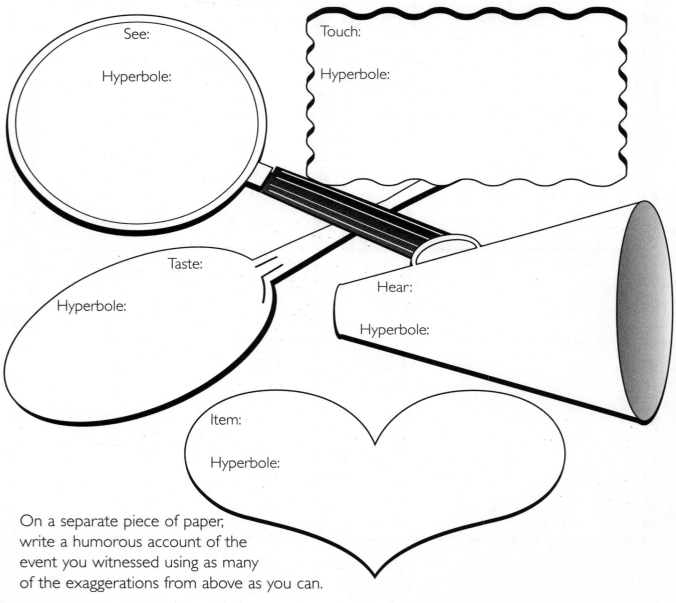

See:

Hyperbole:

Touch:

Hyperbole:

Taste:

Hyperbole:

Hear:

Hyperbole:

Item:

Hyperbole:

On a separate piece of paper, write a humorous account of the event you witnessed using as many of the exaggerations from above as you can.

Description

Skill: *Write a clear description of an object.*

Overview

When skilled writers describe an object, character, or setting, they "paint a picture with words," helping the reader see an image of the object in his or her mind. When painting a picture with words, writers must include a sufficient amount of informative detail. Noting special features, using descriptive words, and including figurative or sensory language brings the object to life.

Model

My Raincoat

Have you ever had a favorite coat? My raincoat is my favorite coat! It's light purple with darker thread outlining the button area, sleeves, seams, and the huge, round pockets on each side. It has oversized, dark purple buttons that makes it look really original. My raincoat flares out a little from my shoulders and goes to just a little below my knees. I wear that coat so much, it is beginning to show signs of wear and tear. I have to admit it has worn elbows, the end of the sleeves look quite dingy, and the collar is frayed. What's worse, it has a big hot chocolate stain near the hem. It's also getting a little small for me and has a slight odor, like a dandelion. I need a new raincoat, but I don't think I'll be able to find another raincoat like it!

How to Teach

Descriptions of objects can be found in literature, but only occasionally are they pure descriptions of the object. Usually, and quite naturally, these descriptions are interspersed with dialogue and plot points. When teaching students to write a description, you can guide them to include specific criteria. For instance, in the model above, the authors included the object, descriptive words, sensory details, and a simile *like a dandelion.* Criteria for the description of an

object may include three or more from the following list. If a student struggles with descriptive writing, differentiate by assigning only one or two from the list.

- details, descriptive words (adjectives showing color, size, shape, and so on)
- senses
- metaphors, similes, or other figurative language

Share the model with your students. Ask *What helps you see a picture of the object?* Have groups write down those words. Show students how to categorize the words they chose under such labels as *details, color, adjectives,* and so on. Explain to them that descriptions only become clear when enough detail is included, and they need to make sure they include the chosen criteria in their writing. If your students seem ready to complete the third graphic organizer, which includes a simile, you may find it necessary to share some other examples, such as *hungry as a bear, slow as a snail, fast as lightning,* and *dark as night.*

Literature Sources for Other Models

Creech, S. (1997). *Chasing redbird.* New York: Scholastic. (See p. 78, dog description & p. 107, bathroom description.)

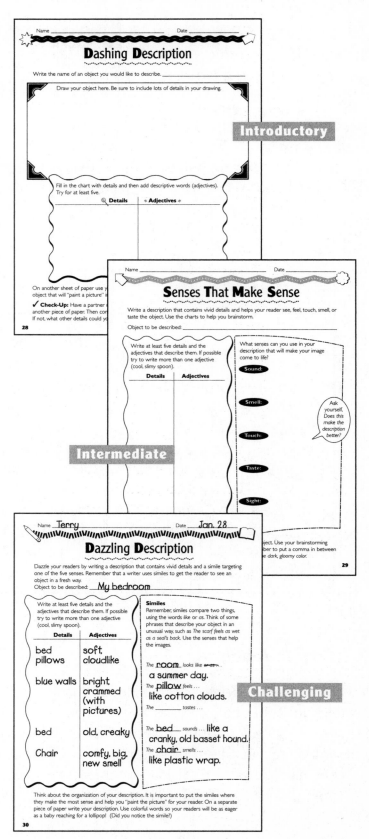

Roberts, W. D. (1996). *Twisted summer.* New York: Aladdin Paperbacks. (See p. 16, character description & p. 48, setting description.)

Howard, E. F. (1991). *Aunt Flossie's hat (and crab cakes later).* New York: Clarion Books. (picture book)

Teacher to Teacher

The best descriptions will be written by following the best model. If you are asking students to include color or taste, please add more information to the model. With the class, ask for suggestions, such as *If we wanted to add the sense of "feel' to this description, what could we write?* Students may suggest *The hot chocolate stain feels stiff and a little sticky.*

Using the Tiered Organizers

When students understand that descriptions need to be clear enough so they can create an image in the readers' mind, they are ready to complete one of the following activities:

Introductory: **Dashing Description**
Students draw a picture of the object and use at least five adjectives and details to describe it.

Intermediate: **Senses That Make Sense**
Students "paint a picture" of their object with descriptive words and sensory details.

Challenging: **Dazzling Description**
Students enrich their descriptions with descriptive words, sensory details, and a simile.

Dashing Description

Write the name of an object you would like to describe. _____

Draw your object here. Be sure to include lots of details in your drawing.

Fill in the chart with details and then add descriptive words (adjectives). Try for at least five.

🔍 **Details**	✱ **Adjectives** ✱

On another sheet of paper use your details and adjectives to write a description of your object that will "paint a picture" in your reader's mind.

✔ **Check-Up:** Have a partner read your description and draw what you have written on another piece of paper. Then compare your drawing with your partner's. Is it the same? If not, what other details could you add to your description?

Senses That Make Sense

Write a description that contains vivid details and helps your reader see, feel, touch, smell, or taste the object. Use the charts to help you brainstorm.

Object to be described: _____

Write at least five details and the adjectives that describe them. If possible try to write more than one adjective (cool, slimy spoon).

Details	Adjectives

What senses can you use in your description that will make your image come to life?

Sound:

Smell:

Touch:

Taste:

Sight:

Ask yourself, *Does this make the description better?*

On a separate piece of paper write a description of your object. Use your brainstorming ideas to help "paint a picture" in your reader's mind. Remember to put a comma in between two adjectives when using two adjectives as in the phrase *the dark, gloomy color.*

Dazzling Description

Dazzle your readers by writing a description that contains vivid details and a simile targeting one of the five senses. Remember that a writer uses similes to get the reader to see an object in a fresh way.

Object to be described: _____

Write at least five details and the adjectives that describe them. If possible try to write more than one adjective (cool, slimy spoon).

Details	Adjectives

Similes

Remember, similes compare two things, using the words *like* or *as*. Think of some phrases that describe your object in an unusual way, such as *The scarf feels as wet as a seal's back.* Use the senses that help the images.

The _____ *looks like or as . . .*

The _____ *feels . . .*

The _____ *tastes . . .*

The _____ *sounds . . .*

The _____ *smells . . .*

Think about the organization of your description. It is important to put the similes where they make the most sense and help you "paint the picture" for your reader. On a separate piece of paper write your description. Use colorful words so your readers will be as eager as a baby reaching for a lollipop! (Did you notice the simile?)

Enumeration

Skill: *Write an annotated list that describes the elements of a person, place, or thing.*

Overview

Enumeration, in its basic form, is a descriptive list, often a series of sentences or paragraphs with key points and details supporting the topic. Enumeration organizes the text for the writer and the reader and gives the reader a clear overview of what is being defined. We see instances of enumeration every day. For instance, an article listing endangered species and then giving details about each one uses enumeration. A brochure that defines "Services Available at Samantha's Surreal Spa" is also enumerative. A description of a character detailing the hair, face, and body in a systematic order employs enumeration.

Model

Welcome to My Beautiful Classroom

There are lots of reasons why I like my classroom. First, it is really big and roomy. We sit at rectangle tables that are about six feet by two feet. Since there are four of us sitting at the table, we have lots of room. The chairs are comfortable. They are bright orange and have matching cushion seats and backs. The floor has a light green rug, which means we don't need tennis balls on the chair legs to keep the noise down. The bulletin boards are neat. They run all the way from the floor to the ceiling, and our teacher writes on them in bright colors. There is a great reading area in our room. It has a blue couch that my teacher said used to be in her apartment. The couch has four comfy pillows: two red, one yellow, and one blue-striped. Next to the couch are lots of books in big, bright-colored baskets, so I never have a problem finding something I like to read. My classroom? It's the best!

How to Teach

Enumeration is best taught after description. Notice how each succeeding sentence in the model becomes a mini-description. To understand enumeration, students must recognize important points, discuss each key point, and stick to the topic. Unlike sequence or chronology, the order of the points does not matter. For example, the model could have begun with the bulletin boards, the rug, or the book baskets and ended with the couch.

Show students that the model lists the components of the classroom. Using a T chart, list the key points: room size, tables, chairs, rug, couch, and book baskets. On the other side of the T chart, list the descriptive details. Your end result will look something like this:

Key Points	Supporting Details
room size	big
tables	6 by 2 feet 4 kids at each table
chairs	orange cushions
rug	light green keeps noise down
couch	blue, 4 pillows
book baskets	big, bright colored lots of books

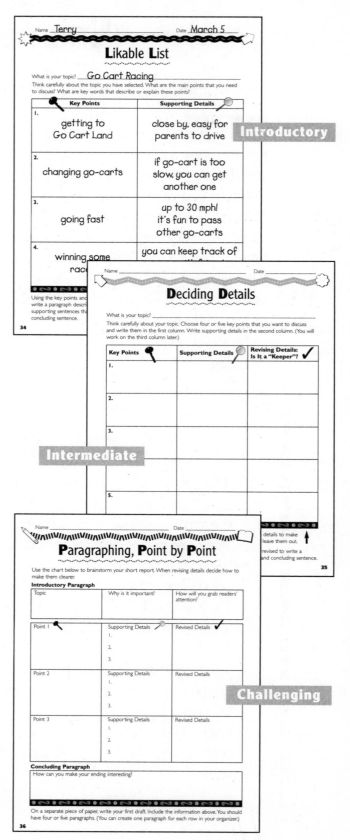

Name Terry   Date March 5

Likable List

What is your topic? Go Cart Racing

Think carefully about the topic you have selected. What are the main points that you need to discuss? What are key words that describe or explain these points?

Key Points	Supporting Details
1. getting to Go Cart Land	close by, easy for parents to drive
2. changing go-carts	if go-cart is too slow, you can get another one
3. going fast	up to 30 mph! it's fun to pass other go-carts
4. winning some race	you can keep track of

Introductory

Using the key points and
write a paragraph descri
supporting sentences tha
concluding sentence.

34

Name _____ Date _____

Deciding Details

What is your topic? _____

Think carefully about your topic. Choose four or five key points that you want to discuss and write them in the first column. Write supporting details in the second column. (You will work on the third column later.)

Key Points	Supporting Details	Revising Details: Is It a "Keeper"? ✓
1.		
2.		
3.		
5.		

Intermediate

details to make
leave them out.

revised to write a
and concluding sentence.

35

Name _____ Date _____

Paragraphing, Point by Point

Use the chart below to brainstorm your short report. When revising details decide how to make them clearer.

Introductory Paragraph

Topic	Why is it important?	How will you grab readers' attention?
Point 1	Supporting Details 1. 2. 3.	Revised Details
Point 2	Supporting Details 1. 2. 3.	Revised Details
Point 3	Supporting Details 1. 2. 3.	Revised Details

Challenging

Concluding Paragraph

How can you make your ending interesting?

On a separate piece of paper, write your first draft. Include the information above. You should have four or five paragraphs. (You can create one paragraph for each row in your organizer.)

36

Referring to this list, ask students what other points about the classroom could have been included. Answers may include wall color, windows, type of door, light fixtures, white board, or chalkboard. Then have them invent some details about these components. Help students recognize that enumeration is a list describing the components of something. When enumerating, they must include the key points and enough detail to ensure that the reader understands the topic. Explain that a report containing the state bird, flag, flower, and anthem would also be enumeration. The list would be the state symbols, and the description of these symbols would be the details. When having your students write a report, be sure to share with them a nonfiction model that exemplifies what you expect of their writing.

Literature Sources for Other Models

Eyewitness Books (such as *Boats, Fish, Shark, Rock and Mineral*—each presents different aspects, usually not in any particular order). New York: Alfred A. Knopf.

Journey Through books (such as *Journey through Japan*). (1991). Mahwah, NJ: Troll.

Cleveland, W., & Alvarez, M. (1994). *Yo, Sacramento! (and all those other state capitals you don't know)*. New York: Scholastic.

Teacher to Teacher

Although the order of the list in enumeration is not important, sometimes a sequence does naturally evolve. For instance, in the model, further description would have naturally followed or preceded the description of size of the table.

Using the Tiered Organizers

When students understand that enumeration is a list that describes the elements of a thing, they are ready for one of the following graphic organizers.

Introductory: **Likable List**
Students outline and write a paragraph on a selected topic by creating a descriptive list with three points and supporting detail.

Intermediate: **Deciding Details**
Students outline and write a descriptive list with four points, each supported by details, and brainstorm alternative ways to describe the details.

Challenging: **Paragraphing, Point by Point**
Students outline and write a short report with three or four points using enumeration. Each point will have at least three details to form a paragraph. The essay will include an introductory paragraph, supporting paragraphs, and a concluding paragraph. (Topics may include four interesting places to visit in your town, three movies worth seeing, five favorite animals in the zoo, or what to see at the school science fair.)

Likable List

What is your topic? _____

Think carefully about the topic you have selected. What are the main points that you need to discuss? What are key words that describe or explain these points?

Key Points	Supporting Details
1.	
2.	
3.	
4.	

Using the key points and supporting details from above, on a separate sheet of paper, write a paragraph describing your topic. Be sure to include a topic sentence, at least two supporting sentences that help your reader understand what you are writing about, and a concluding sentence.

Deciding Details

What is your topic? _____

Think carefully about your topic. Choose four or five key points that you want to discuss and write them in the first column. Write supporting details in the second column. (You will work on the third column later.)

Key Points	Supporting Details	Revising Details: Is It a "Keeper"?
1.		
2.		
3.		
4.		
5.		

Carefully reread the supporting details. In the third column revise the details to make a clearer statement. If you notice details that may confuse the reader, leave them out.

On a separate piece of paper, use the key points and the details you revised to write a paragraph describing your topic. Be sure to include a topic sentence and concluding sentence.

Paragraphing, Point by Point

Use the chart below to brainstorm your short report. When revising details decide how to make them clearer.

Introductory Paragraph

Topic	Why is it important?	How will you grab readers' attention?
Point 1	Supporting Details 1. 2. 3.	Revised Details
Point 2	Supporting Details 1. 2. 3.	Revised Details
Point 3	Supporting Details 1. 2. 3.	Revised Details

Concluding Paragraph

How can you make your ending interesting?

On a separate piece of paper, write your first draft. Include the information above. You should have four or five paragraphs. (You can create one paragraph for each row in your organizer.)

Persuasive Essay

Skill: *State an opinion and provide evidence that convinces others that the opinion is correct.*

Overview

If you have ever tried to talk someone into doing something or believing that your opinion is correct, you have had experience with persuasion. In order for writing to be persuasive, the writer needs to take a stand on an issue and then use logical reasons and relevant details to convince readers that the stand is correct and justified.

Model

Less Homework by Jack Conway

(an appeal from a student to members of the local school committee)

I think teachers should be required to limit the amount of homework they give each night. Many of us spend hours after school completing homework assignments. There are several reasons why I believe it would be a good idea to limit the amount of homework we receive. If we had less homework, it would give us time to enjoy sports and other activities after school. As it is now, knowing we have hours of homework to do when we get done with the activities makes it hard to concentrate on what we're doing and takes the fun out of them. Less homework would also mean that we could cut down on the number of books we have to lug home in our backpacks. Fewer books to carry would reduce the strain the heavy books are placing on our shoulders and backs. With fewer homework assignments, teachers would have less homework to correct the next day. They could spend more time having fun, planning lessons, or relaxing. They would always be in a good mood. Some people might argue that having more homework makes kids smarter. I agree this sounds like it would make sense, but in reality I know that my brain can only absorb so much. Doing more doesn't always mean learning more. As you can see, there are several very good reasons why teachers should be required to limit the number of homework assignments each night.

How to Teach

Read the model essay aloud and then reread the title and the line that follows it. Point out that this student has written the essay with specific readers in mind (members of the local school committee). As you review the model with students, note how Jack has tailored his comments to this particular audience. Remind them that the function of

a persuasive essay is to sway a reader, so the more closely the supporting details match the reader's interests and appeal to their concerns (e.g., student physical well being), the more effective the essay is likely to be. Make sure to give students an opportunity to consider their audience before they begin to construct an argument in their own persuasive essay.

Write the topic sentence from the model across the top of a piece of chart paper and help students see that this sentence introduces Jack's stand on the amount of homework given each night. Next, have students identify the three reasons Jack gives to support his stand and list them. Be sure to leave space under each reason to note how Jack elaborated on each reason.

Sometimes students worry that they will weaken their argument if they include information that contradicts their position. Actually, the opposite is true, provided they can explain why this opposing information is not convincing. In the model above, ask students to identify the sentence that gives information contradicting the argument ("Some people might argue that having more homework makes kids smarter"). Help students see that the following two sentences are really supporting Jack's argument for less homework. (He contends that the quantity of work does not help kids get any smarter; instead it wears them out.) Next, have pairs of students brainstorm other possible arguments those who oppose less homework could use. Challenge them to convince the class that these supporting arguments would not be justified or valid.

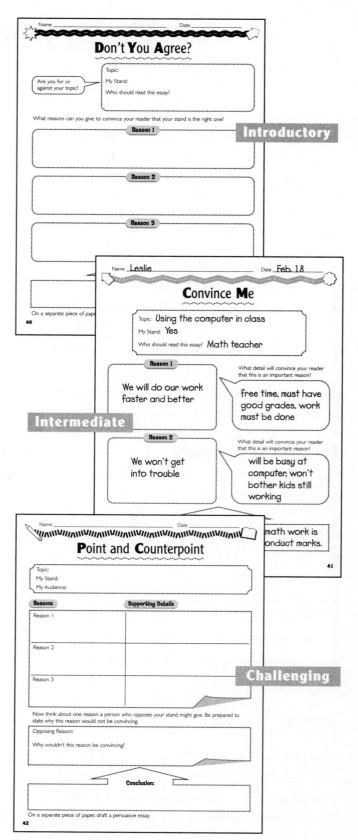

Finally, steer students away from clichéd conclusions like "The End." Teach them other strategies for writing conclusions. Point out, for example, that in the model the author connects the end of the essay to the beginning to provide closure. As a next step, you may want to ask students to revise a piece from their writing folder using this conclusion strategy.

Literature Sources for Other Models

Babbitt, N. (1975). *Tuck everlasting*. New York: Farrar, Straus & Giroux (See Ch. 12, in which Tuck convinces Winnie not to tell anyone about the spring.)

Scieszka, J. (1989). *The true story of the 3 little pigs*. New York: Puffin Books. (The wolf tries to convince everyone he's innocent.)

Teacher to Teacher

We find it easier for students to write persuasive essays after they have had opportunities to discuss their topic and brainstorm possible reasons that substantiate their stand.

Using the Tiered Organizers

When students are able to take a stand on an issue and give logical reasons to defend their position, they are ready to be matched to one of the following graphic organizers:

Introductory: **Don't You Agree?**
Students take a stand on an issue, determine the audience, provide three logical reasons to support their stand, and include a concluding statement. On a separate paper, students can write one sentence from each section of the graphic organizer to create a basic five-sentence paragraph, which can then be further developed.

Intermediate: **Convince Me**
Students take a stand on an issue and determine their audience. They provide at least two logical reasons to support their stand, elaborate on each reason, and include a concluding statement. On a separate piece of paper, students draft a persuasive essay using the graphic organizer.

Challenging: **Point and Counterpoint**
Students complete the steps for the intermediate level. In addition, they provide one reason that people who oppose their stand could cite and explain why this reason may not be valid. On a separate piece of paper, students draft a persuasive essay, using the organizer.

Don't You Agree?

Are you for or against your topic?

Topic:

My Stand:

Who should read this essay?

What reasons can you give to convince your reader that your stand is the right one?

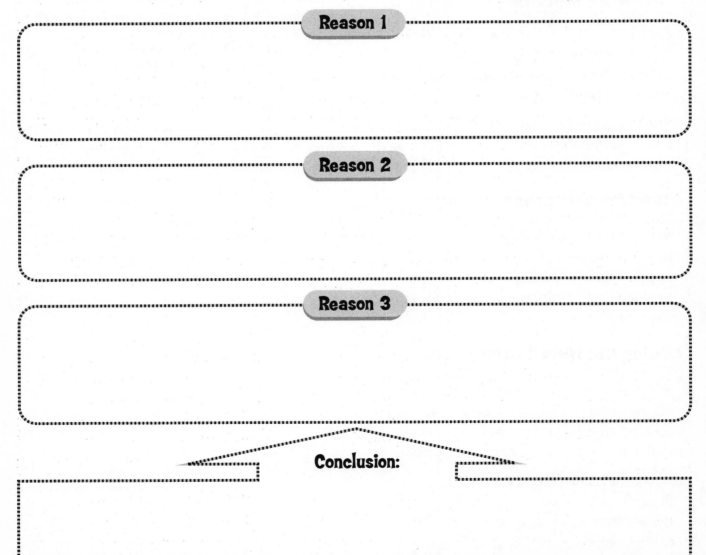

Reason 1

Reason 2

Reason 3

Conclusion:

On a separate piece of paper, draft a persuasive essay.

Convince Me

Topic:

My Stand:

Who should read this essay?

Reason 1

What detail will convince your reader that this is an important reason?

Reason 2

What detail will convince your reader that this is an important reason?

Conclusion:

On a separate piece of paper, draft a persuasive essay.

Point and Counterpoint

Topic:

My Stand:

My Audience:

Reasons	Supporting Details
Reason 1	
Reason 2	
Reason 3	

Now think about one reason a person who opposes your stand might give. Be prepared to state why this reason would not be convincing.

Opposing Reason:

Why wouldn't this reason be convincing?

Conclusion:

On a separate piece of paper, draft a persuasive essay.

Compare and Contrast Essay

Skill: *Determine similarities and differences in objects, settings, events, or characters.*

Overview

Compare means to look at similarities, while contrast means to focus on differences. Writers often compare and contrast objects, settings, events, and characters. They do this to add details, present information, or foreshadow events. Sometimes authors identify specific categories against which they compare and contrast these objects, settings, events, and characters.

Model

Taylor Jenkins and Samantha Thompson have been best friends for five years, since kindergarten. They have a great deal in common. Both girls are ten years old and have two younger brothers. When they are together, they like to shop at the mall and listen to music. Just last month, Taylor and Sam decided to get their ears pierced. Afterwards, they walked around the mall, showing off their new jewelry. Although they spend a lot of time together, Taylor and Samantha do not have the same personalities or enjoy all the same activities.

Taylor, for example, never sits still. Her long, brown hair, which is usually tied in a ponytail, is always in motion. She is on two soccer teams, a town team and a traveling team. She usually plays forward and she likes that position, especially when she scores a goal or two. Taylor likes to win, but losing doesn't bother her. She always has a smile—win or lose. Maybe that's why everyone likes to be around her.

Sam, on the other hand, is not nearly as outgoing as Taylor. In fact, she tends to be shy around people she doesn't know very well. She tries to avoid competitive team sports. When Taylor and Sam aren't together, you can probably find Sam with her nose in a good book. She is happy to spend hours devouring the latest Harry Potter or catching up on one of Katherine Patterson's novels. Taylor and Sam would agree that best friends don't have to be matching bookends, but they have to like spending time together doing what they both enjoy.

How to Teach

If students are just learning to compare and contrast, you might want to allow two or three periods to present this lesson on writing a three-paragraph compare-contrast piece. Refer students to the following diagram and the compare-contrast model on page 43.

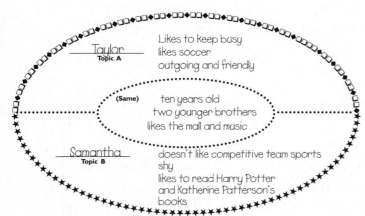

Beginning with the center circle (the common features), explain how to use the notes in this section to write the first paragraph. Demonstrate how to create complete sentences that show how Taylor and Samantha are alike. In the next lesson, revisit the graphic organizer and model how to move from the outer two parts of the organizer to the next two paragraphs, contrasting the girls.

Ask students to identify the categories they could use to compare and contrast the topics. For example, in the model, we consider age, siblings, personalities, and interests. Brainstorm other possible categories, such as favorite foods or movies, and work collaboratively to revise the model essay, comparing and contrasting Taylor and Samantha with

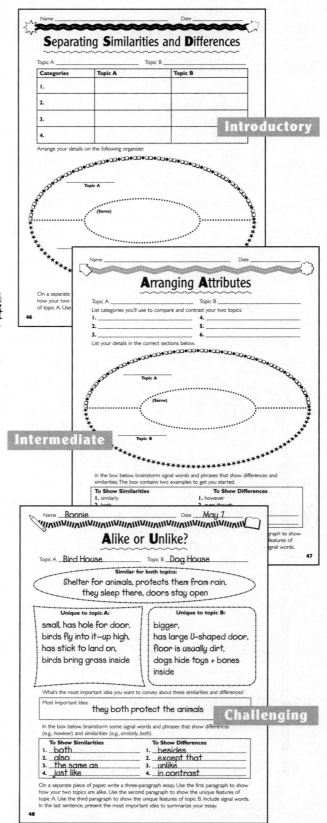

these other categories in mind. Finally, talk about the use of transition words and phrases in the model that signal contrast (*although, on the other hand*) and the way the final sentence finishes off the essay by capturing the main idea.

Literature Sources for Other Models

Gardiner, J. R. (1980). *Stone Fox*. New York: Trumpet Club. (Compare the characters: Willy and Stone Fox.)

MacLachlan, P. (1985). *Sarah, plain and tall*. New York: Trumpet Club. (Compare the settings: Maine and the prairie.)

Steptoe, J. (1987). *Mufaro's beautiful daughters: An African tale*. New York: Lothrop, Lee & Shepard Books. (See Teacher to Teacher, below.)

Kurtz, J. (2000). *Faraway home*. San Diego, CA: Gulliver Books. (picture book)

Teacher to Teacher

You may want to spend time sharing examples of literature in which the compare-contrast text structure is evident. Discuss why the author identifies similarities and differences. For example, *Mufaro's Beautiful Daughters* begins with contrasting descriptions of Manyara and Nyasha, the two daughters. Steptoe uses the contrast to develop character traits and foreshadow plot.

Using the Tiered Organizers

Once students can brainstorm and organize similarities and differences between objects, settings, events, or people, they are ready to be introduced to the following activities. In each, they brainstorm similarities and differences for two topics in preparation for writing a three-paragraph compare-contrast essay.

Introductory: **Separating Similarities and Differences**
Students identify categories they can use to compare and contrast two objects, settings, events, or characters.

Intermediate: **Arranging Attributes**
Students complete the same activities as above and then brainstorm possible words and phrases that signal similarities and differences.

Challenging: **Alike or Unlike?**
Students brainstorm similarities and differences for two topics and signal words that show these relationships. Next, they identify the most important idea about the topic and draft a final sentence that presents it.

Separating **S**imilarities and **D**ifferences

Topic A _____ Topic B _____

Categories	Topic A	Topic B
1.		
2.		
3.		
4.		

Arrange your details on the following organizer.

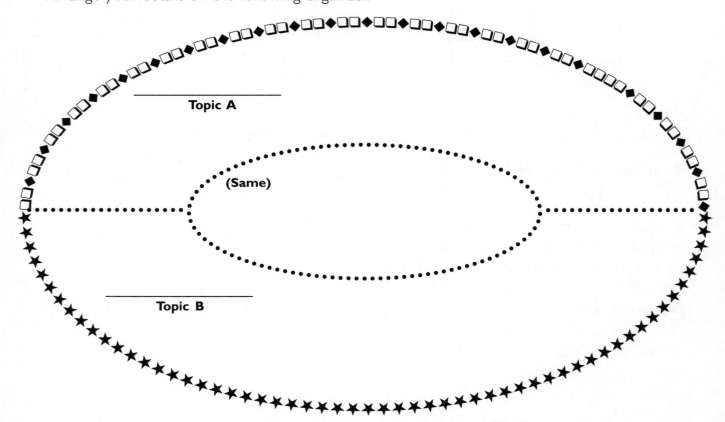

Topic A

(Same)

Topic B

On a separate piece of paper, write a three-paragraph essay. Use the first paragraph to show how your two topics are alike. Use the second paragraph to show the unique characteristics of topic A. Use the third paragraph to show the unique characteristics of topic B.

Arranging Attributes

Topic A _____   Topic B _____

List categories you'll use to compare and contrast your two topics:

1. _____   **4.** _____

2. _____   **5.** _____

3. _____   **6.** _____

List your details in the correct sections below.

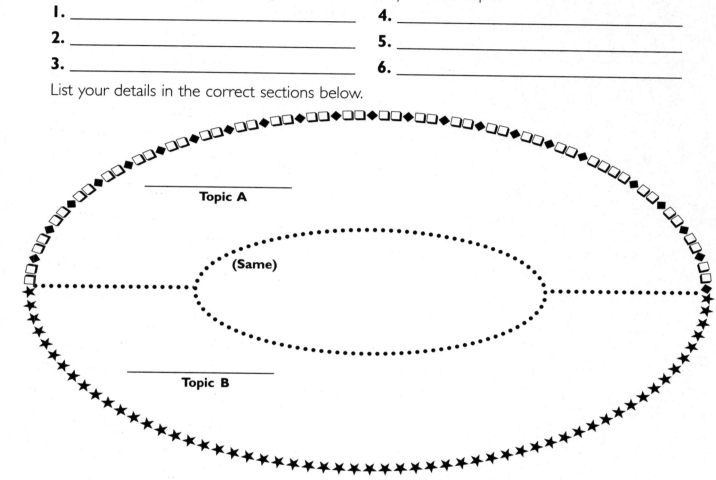

Topic A

(Same)

Topic B

In the box below, brainstorm signal words and phrases that show differences and similarities. The box contains two examples to get you started.

To Show Similarities	To Show Differences
1. similarly	**1.** however
2. both	**2.** even though
3. _____	**3.** _____
4. _____	**4.** _____

On a separate piece of paper, write a three-paragraph essay. Use the first paragraph to show how your two topics are alike. Use the second paragraph to show the unique features of topic A. Use the third paragraph to show the unique features of topic B. Use signal words.

Alike or **U**nlike?

Topic A _____ Topic B _____

Similar for both topics:

Unique to topic A:

Unique to topic B:

What's the most important idea you want to convey about these similarities and differences?

Most Important Idea:

In the box below, brainstorm some signal words and phrases that show differences (e.g., *however*) and similarities (e.g., *similarly*, *both*).

To Show Similarities	**To Show Differences**
1. _____	1. _____
2. _____	2. _____
3. _____	3. _____
4. _____	4. _____

On a separate piece of paper, write a three-paragraph essay. Use the first paragraph to show how your two topics are alike. Use the second paragraph to show the unique features of topic A. Use the third paragraph to show the unique features of topic B. Include signal words. In the last sentence, present the most important idea to summarize your essay.

Informative How-To Essay

Skill: *Write sequential and detailed directions explaining how to do something.*

Overview

Being able to explain how to do something is a life skill. It requires being able to understand sequence, distinguish between important and extraneous information, and choose appropriate words. For instance, when explaining how to make an ice cream sundae, *put the ice cream in a bowl* must come after *scoop out the ice cream*. The order is extremely important, correct details a must, and precise vocabulary essential.

Model

How to Put a Ring on Your Finger

Decide on which finger you want to wear the ring. Pick up the ring in the hand opposite the one you want to wear it on. For example, if you plan to put the ring on your right hand, pick the ring up with your left hand. Pick up the ring between your thumb and one or two fingers, making sure the empty circle of the ring faces the other hand. Next, hold the ring tightly and bring the finger you want to wear it on toward the ring. Then, glide the finger into the opening of the ring. Finally, make sure the ring goes past the knuckle on the ring finger. You should now have the ring on your finger. You may want to check to make sure that the ring is not so loose that it can slide off your finger. Enjoy wearing your ring.

How to Teach

When you teach writing the how-to, it is fun to model students' directions. Once we saw a teacher who was following a student's written directions literally. The teacher read *Put ice cream in a bowl* and put a carton of ice cream on top of the bowl. *Put chocolate sauce all around* resulted in a trail of chocolate sauce around the outside of the bowl (landing on a trash bag the talented teacher had put on the table prior to the lesson).

When students successfully revised their directions to give their reader clarity and specificity, they made and ate an ice cream sundae. Students learned the importance of writing directions in order, with detail, and in clear language. A similar lesson can focus on explaining precisely how to make a peanut butter and jelly sandwich, pop corn in the microwave, or put extra toppings on a pizza.

If possible, start with a "hands on" experience prior to sharing the model, "How to Put a Ring on Your Finger." Explain to students that they are starting with a simple exercise so that eventually they can write more complex directions for things they actually do, such as giving a friend directions to the mall. Then have students read the model carefully. Let them use a plastic ring to try out the directions, or at least have them pretend and go through the steps of putting on a ring. They should be successful! Discuss all the reasons why this how-to was easy to follow. Notice the sequence of steps. Ask students if they see any signal words that help establish the order of the directions (*next*, *then*, and *finally*). Note the details in the explanation. In the end, you may point out that the author also wants the reader to check to make sure the ring is not too loose. Ensure that students understand the criteria of a well-written how-to: it must be in sequential order and include signal words, detail, and precise vocabulary. Look back at the model and discuss these four points.

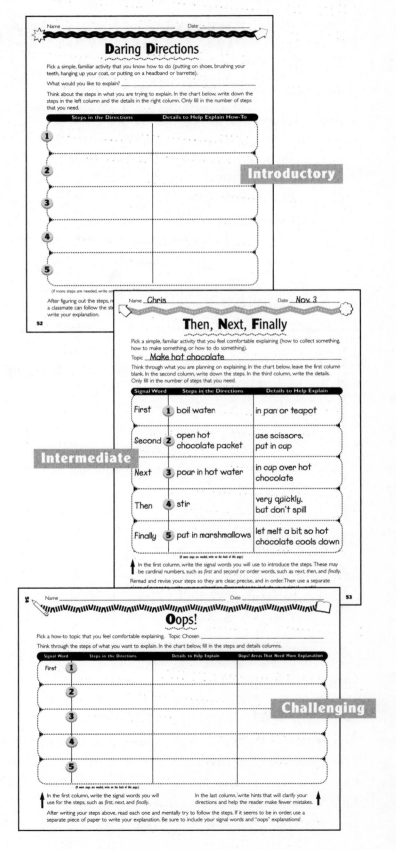

Literature Sources for Other Models

Thomas, J., Pagel, D., & Thomas, D. (1998). *The ultimate book of kid concoctions: More than 65 wacky, wild and crazy concoctions.* Strongville, OH: Kid Concoction Company.

Sadler, J., & Bradford, J. (2000). *Making fleece crafts (kids can do it).* New York: Kids Can Press.

Any Klutz book (*What can you do with a paper bag?, The buck book, Cat's cradle, Face painting*). New York: Scholastic.

Teacher to Teacher

The problems most students have when writing directions are making sure all steps are included and thoroughly explained. When possible have students try out their own directions and then let a partner try to follow them. It's amazing how something that is quite ordinary and simple to do can be so difficult to explain.

Using the Tiered Organizers

When students can explain orally how to do something in the correct order and with the necessary details, they are ready for one of the following graphic organizers. With each, encourage students to select a familiar activity or skill to explain.

Introductory: **Daring Directions**
Students outline steps and details in preparation for writing a how-to.

Intermediate: **Then, Next, Finally**
Students outline steps and details in preparation for writing a how-to and use signal words for the sequence.

Challenging: **Oops!**
Students outline a how-to, using signal words and details. They pinpoint areas that could be confusing, and clarify their directions.

Daring Directions

Pick a simple, familiar activity that you know how to do (putting on shoes, brushing your teeth, hanging up your coat, or putting on a headband or barrette).

What would you like to explain? _____

Think about the steps in what you are trying to explain. In the chart below, write down the steps in the left column and the details in the right column. Only fill in the number of steps that you need.

Steps in the Directions	Details to Help Explain How-To
1	
2	
3	
4	
5	

(If more steps are needed, write on the back of this page.)

After figuring out the steps, read and mentally try to follow them. If you are successful, see if a classmate can follow the steps. If it seems to be in order, use a separate piece of paper to write your explanation.

Then, Next, Finally

Pick a simple, familiar activity that you feel comfortable explaining (how to collect something, how to make something, or how to do something).

Topic _____

Think through what you are planning on explaining. In the chart below, leave the first column blank. In the second column, write down the steps. In the third column, write the details. Only fill in the number of steps that you need.

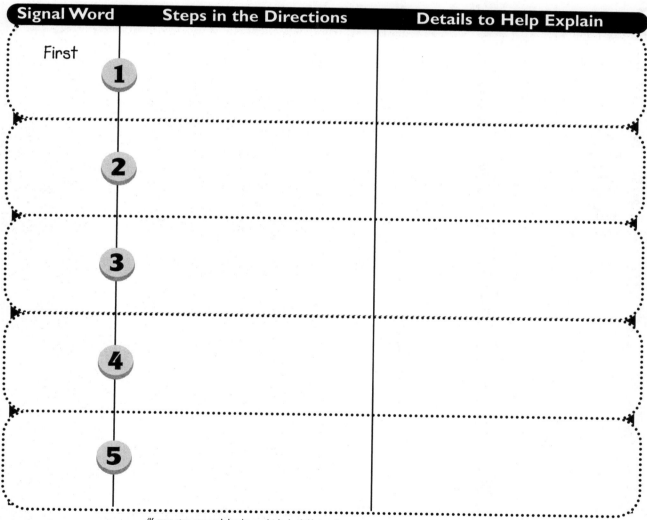

Signal Word	Steps in the Directions	Details to Help Explain
First **1**		
2		
3		
4		
5		

(If more steps are needed, write on the back of this page.)

In the first column, write the signal words you will use to introduce the steps. These may be cardinal numbers, such as *first* and *second* or order words, such as *next*, *then*, and *finally*.

Reread and revise your steps so they are clear, precise, and in order. Then use a separate piece of paper to write your explanation. Remember to include your signal words!

Name _____

Date _____

Oops!

Pick a how-to topic that you feel comfortable explaining. Topic Chosen _____

Think through the steps of what you want to explain. In the chart below, fill in the steps and details columns.

Signal Word	Steps in the Directions	Details to Help Explain	Oops! Areas That Need More Explanation
First ①			
②			
③			
④			
⑤			

(If more steps are needed, write on the back of this page.)

← In the first column, write the signal words you will use for the steps, such as *first*, *next*, and *finally*.

In the last column, write hints that will clarify your directions and help the reader make fewer mistakes.

After writing your steps above, read each one and mentally try to follow the steps. If it seems to be in order, use a separate piece of paper to write your explanation. Be sure to include your signal words and "oops" explanations!

Point of View

Skill: *Write a paragraph that relates an incident or experience from different points of view.*

Overview

A narrative may tell a story or recount an event. In a narrative the writer relates what happened, includes details, and employs descriptive words that help the reader see and feel what is happening. Narratives are usually written in the first person (in which one or more main character tells the story from a personal perspective, using the pronouns *I* or *we*), or in the third person (in which a narrator who is not involved in the story, tells it as an onlooker, using the pronouns *he*, *she*, or *they*). A narrative should include enough surprises to keep the reader captivated. This can be done by foreshadowing, including interesting details, qualifying a character in some way, such as *always in trouble*, or with an unexpected ending.

Model

FIRST-PERSON NARRATIVE

Blade Skating Is Supposed to Be Fun

My friend Cassie and I went blade skating last week. We decided it would be a great idea to roller blade up to Meadowbrook for an ice cream. Getting there was fun until Cassie lost one of her wheels and she couldn't skate right. The sidewalk was hot and she didn't have any shoes! Well, we decided to carry the one roller blade, then Cassie held on to me and I pulled her to the ice cream stand. It worked out okay, but Cassie had to keep putting down her left foot to keep her balance and the sidewalk was burning hot! By the time we got to the stand, her left foot was hurting. Cassie took off her roller blade and hopped on the right foot to get her ice cream. Unfortunately, when she jumped to the table her ice cream fell off! Cassie looked at the ice cream splattered on the cement and then plopped her sore foot right into it for instant relief! Luckily, the ice cream clerk gave Cassie another ice cream!

THIRD-PERSON NARRATIVE

Carlos' Hike With a View

Carlos hiked happily up the mountain. He lived in the city and had never been on a mountain hike before. He walked slowly, not because he was tired, but because he wanted to notice and remember everything. He felt the cool air on his face and was glad he wore his heaviest sweatshirt. He looked at the surrounding trees and began mentally to label the colors: red, orange, kind of purple, brown, and green. He listened to the sound his shoes made as he walked on the fallen leaves and twigs. Carlos made a decision right then and there. Someday, when he was a grownup, he would live in the mountains.

How to Teach

When initially teaching narrative, it may be important to familiarize students with story elements (character, setting, problem, and solution), but not all narratives include every story component ("Carlos' Hike With a View" does not have a problem or a solution). It is also important to teach them to choose a perspective from which to tell the story. Use the models above to explain the elements of a narrative. Then select other models of the narrative type the students are learning to write. Read each one with the class and have students identify the story elements (if they are present), as well as what "grabbed" them as they listened. Help students notice that while perspective may change from story to story the other criteria remain the same for either a first-person or third-person narrative.

When students write their own narratives, encourage them to think about an incident they would like to share, the main events of the incident, and how they can keep their readers captivated. Have students also consider how they might best tell the story— with a first-person narrator or a more removed third-person narrator. Remind students that good narratives use lots of details and captivate the reader by hinting at what is to come, describing with a qualifier the character or the incident, or including an unexpected ending.

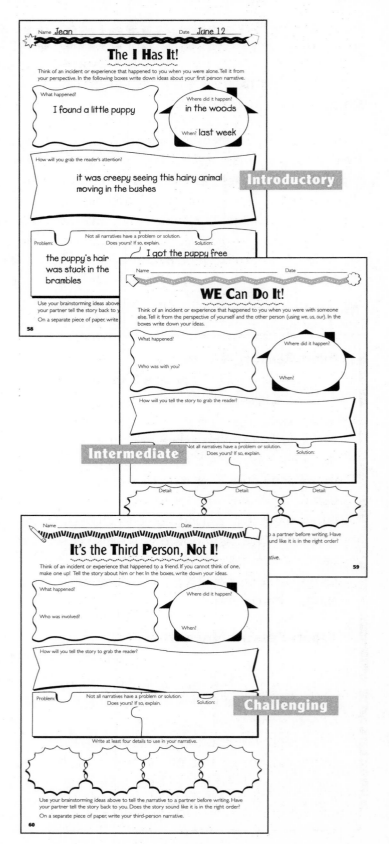

Literature Sources for Other Models

First Person:
Hesse, K. (1997). *Out of the dust.*
New York: Scholastic Press.

Taylor, M. D. (1976). *Roll of thunder, hear my cry.* New York: Bantam Books.

Third Person:
Lord, B. B. (1984). *In the year of the boar and Jackie Robinson.* New York: Harper Trophy.

Paulsen, G. (1985). *DogSong.* New York: Puffin Books.

Teacher to Teacher

You may find it easier to start with a first-person narrative, since children have grown up telling *I* stories. As students add more characters to their *I* narratives, they begin the transition to the third-person voice, including *he* or *she* in the narrative. It is helpful to have students tell their narrative orally to a partner prior to actually writing. If students need more support, revisit the writing-paragraphs and voice sections of this book.

Using the Tiered Organizers

When students can identify the details and components that help a narrative captivate the reader, they are ready for one of the following graphic organizers.

Introductory: **The *I* Has It!**
Students write a first-person narrative about an incident or experience in their life when they were alone, including an element that captivates the reader.

Intermediate: **We Can Do It!**
Students will write a first-person narrative about an incident or experience that happened in their life when they were with someone else, including at least three details and an element that captivates the reader.

Challenging: **It's the Third Person, Not *I*!**
Students write a third-person narrative about an incident or experience that happened to one or two other people, including at least four details and an element that captivates the reader.

The I Has It!

Think of an incident or experience that happened to you when you were alone. Tell it from your perspective. In the following boxes write down ideas about your first person narrative.

What happened?

Where did it happen?

When?

How will you grab the reader's attention?

Problem:

Not all narratives have a problem or solution.
Does yours? If so, explain.

Solution:

Use your brainstorming ideas above to tell the narrative to a partner before writing. Have your partner tell the story back to you. Does the story sound like it is in the right order?

On a separate piece of paper, write your first-person narrative.

WE Can Do It!

Think of an incident or experience that happened to you when you were with someone else. Tell it from the perspective of yourself and the other person (using *we, us, our*). In the boxes write down your ideas.

What happened?

Who was with you?

Where did it happen?

When?

How will you tell the story to grab the reader?

Problem:

Not all narratives have a problem or solution.
Does yours? If so, explain.

Solution:

Detail:

Detail:

Detail:

Use your brainstorming ideas above to tell the narrative to a partner before writing. Have your partner tell the story back to you. Does the story sound like it is in the right order? Can your partner recognize the problem and solution?

On a separate piece of paper, write your first-person narrative.

It's the **Third Person, Not I!**

Think of an incident or experience that happened to a friend. If you cannot think of one, make one up! Tell the story about him or her. In the boxes, write down your ideas.

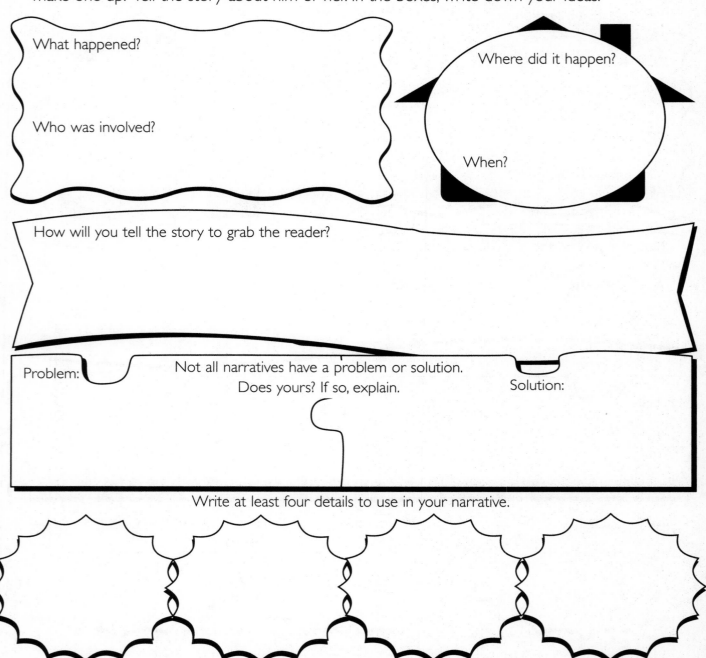

What happened?

Who was involved?

Where did it happen?

When?

How will you tell the story to grab the reader?

Problem:

Not all narratives have a problem or solution. Does yours? If so, explain.

Solution:

Write at least four details to use in your narrative.

Use your brainstorming ideas above to tell the narrative to a partner before writing. Have your partner tell the story back to you. Does the story sound like it is in the right order?

On a separate piece of paper, write your third-person narrative.

Character Development

Overview

Characters often make a story, and a good character description includes both the appearance and personality of the character. Writers develop a character's personality through action and thought. When we discuss character development and description, we need to consider both the appearance (outside characteristics) and the personality (inside characteristics). Although the two can most certainly be defined separately, a character's personality affects the character's appearance. Similarly, the character's appearance may also affect the character's personality. To complicate character development even further, both the character's personality and the plot guide the actions of the character.

Model

Samantha

Samantha's long black hair curled carelessly around her face. Her small dark, brown eyes peered out angrily beneath her uneven bangs. Her tall, thin body stiffened. Like a girl possessed, Samantha ran up the stairs, long legs flying. She knew now wasn't the time but thought to herself, "I'll get him all right!" She could be patient. She would wait for the perfect time to get the little brat back. Samantha hated to be angry, but sometimes her little brother really irritated her.

How to Teach

Explain that narratives often give clues about a character's personality, and the thoughts and actions indicate that personality. For instance, *The young man often helped people in his neighborhood* suggests that the young man is kind. Read the model aloud with the class and ask what words describe Samantha. List students'

answers on the board, categorizing them under appearance (outside) or personality (inside). Ask students to state the personality traits, actions, and thoughts that reflect these traits. The board, showing Samantha's traits, should look something like this:

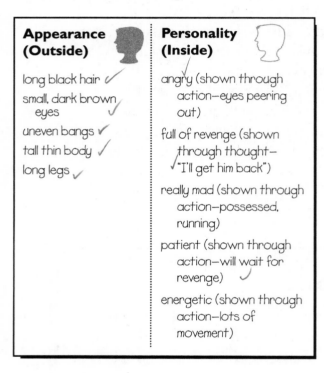

Appearance (Outside)

long black hair ✓
small, dark brown eyes ✓
uneven bangs ✓
tall thin body ✓
long legs ✓

Personality (Inside)

angry (shown through action—eyes peering out)

full of revenge (shown through thought— "I'll get him back")

really mad (shown through action—possessed, running)

patient (shown through action—will wait for revenge) ✓

energetic (shown through action—lots of movement)

Ask students to tell you the components of a good character description. Answers may include appearance, personality, details, and feelings implied through thoughts and actions.

If you feel students are developmentally ready, ask if they can explain what the phrase "like a girl possessed" means. Lead them to see that this simile expresses Samantha's anger. The author uses exaggeration so readers will know just how angry Samantha is.

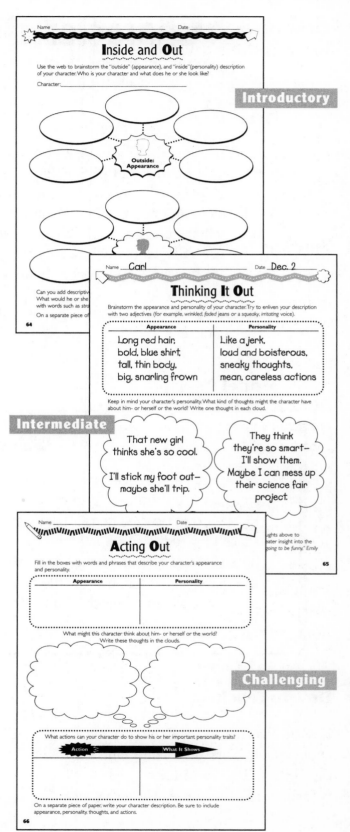

Inside and Out

Use the web to brainstorm the "outside" (appearance), and "inside" (personality) description of your character. Who is your character and what does he or she look like?

Character: _____

Outside: Appearance

Introductory

Thinking It Out

Name: Carl   Date: Dec. 2

Brainstorm the appearance and personality of your character. Try to enliven your description with two adjectives (for example, *wrinkled, faded* jeans or a *squeaky, irritating* voice).

Appearance	Personality
Long red hair, bold, blue shirt, tall, thin body, big, snarling frown	Like a jerk, loud and boisterous, sneaky thoughts, mean, careless actions

Keep in mind your character's personality. What kind of thoughts might the character have about him- or herself or the world? Write one thought in each cloud.

Intermediate

That new girl thinks she's so cool.
I'll stick my foot out— maybe she'll trip.

They think they're so smart— I'll show them. Maybe I can mess up their science fair project.

Acting Out

Name: _____   Date: _____

Fill in the boxes with words and phrases that describe your character's appearance and personality.

Appearance	Personality

What might this character think about him- or herself or the world? Write these thoughts in the clouds.

Challenging

What actions can your character do to show his or her important personality traits?

Action   What It Shows

On a separate piece of paper, write your character description. Be sure to include appearance, personality, thoughts, and actions.

Literature Sources for Other Models

Bauer, J. (2000). *Hope was here.* New York: Scholastic.

Peck, R. (2000). *A year down yonder.* New York: Dial Books.

Gantos, J. (2000). *Joey Pigza loses control.* New York: Scholastic.

Teacher to Teacher

The most difficult aspect of character description and development is not only writing a clear description but also including subtle character traits that are evidenced through thoughts and actions. Students should understand that the character's actions often reflect the character's personality. As they study examples of great narrative writing they will become astute at identifying traits and the actions that complement those traits. For example, they will realize it doesn't make sense if "Honest Jane" decides to steal someone's lunch money. Developments in the character will imply that "Honest Jane" is not honest, or a development in the plot will force her to act in desperation.

Using the Tiered Organizers

When students grasp the concept that writers describe a character through both appearance and personality (thought and action), they are ready for the following graphic organizers.

Introductory: **Inside and Out**
Students brainstorm the appearance and personality of a character and write a description.

Intermediate: **Thinking It Out**
Students write a character description that includes appearance, personality, and thoughts.

Challenging: **Acting Out**
Students enrich their character descriptions for "Thinking It Out" by adding action. Have them include a simile that describes one of the actions for an additional challenge.

Inside and Out

Use the web to brainstorm the "outside" (appearance), and "inside"(personality) description of your character. Who is your character and what does he or she look like?

Character:_____

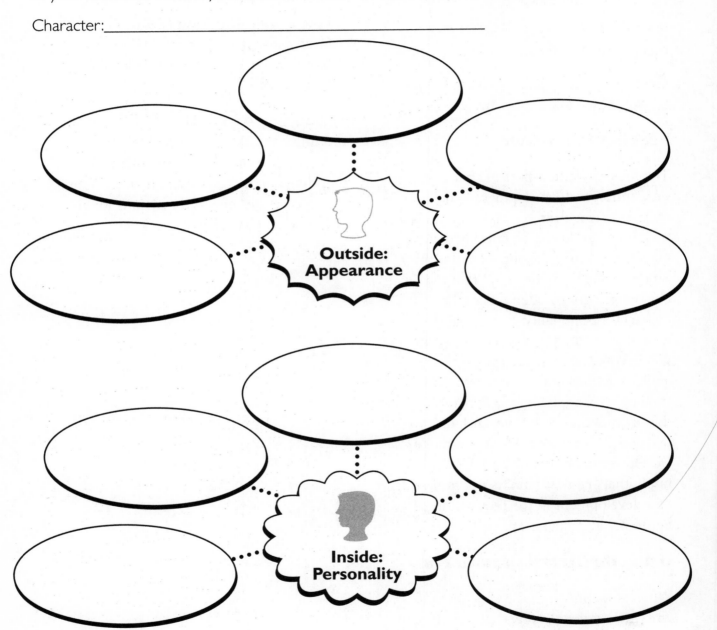

Can you add descriptive words to your web? Think again of the person you are creating. What would he or she look like? If you wrote something like "black hair," describe it further with words such as *straight* and *limp* to give your readers a better picture.

On a separate piece of paper, write your character description using complete sentences.

Thinking It Out

Brainstorm the appearance and personality of your character. Try to enliven your description with two adjectives (for example, *wrinkled, faded* jeans or a *squeaky, irritating* voice).

Appearance	Personality

Keep in mind your character's personality. What kind of thoughts might the character have about him- or herself or the world? Write one thought in each cloud.

On a separate sheet of paper, use your descriptive words and the thoughts above to write a description of your character. Remember, thoughts give you greater insight into the character's personality. Use quotes for thoughts (for example, "*This is going to be funny,*" Emily *thought to herself*).

Acting Out

Fill in the boxes with words and phrases that describe your character's appearance and personality.

Appearance	Personality

What might this character think about him- or herself or the world?
Write these thoughts in the clouds.

What actions can your character do to show his or her important personality traits?

Action ⟩⟩ **What It Shows**

On a separate piece of paper, write your character description. Be sure to include appearance, personality, thoughts, and actions.

Plot Development

Skill: *Organize and fully develop the plot of a story to include rising action and a solution.*

Overview

Plot includes the problems, solutions, and resolution of a story. While students may be able to tell you the components of a story (characters, setting, problem, solution, and resolution), what students may not see as important are the steps between the problem and solution, usually identified as "attempts to solve." The focal point of the plot is not the listing of these components but the rising action with each attempt. A well-developed plot keeps us reading. Obviously the development of the plot is less intense for our student writers than it is for John Grisham. Nonetheless, we can help them learn to develop their stories at an appropriate level.

Model

Sarah walked up to the check-out counter and looked at the list. She didn't want to forget anything. This was the first time Mom had let Sarah come to the store on her own, and she didn't want to mess it up. Sarah was excited in another way, too. She felt like a grownup; after all, she was doing grownup work! She had everything: can of beans, lettuce, milk, and bread.

Sarah got to the cashier and took out the twenty-dollar bill her mother had given her. The cashier looked at her funny. Sarah looked in her hand. Like an idiot, she was was handing the cashier the grocery list instead of the twenty-dollar bill! Sarah reached into her pocket for the twenty. She pushed her hand down deeper. Nothing was there. Frantically, Sarah searched in her other pockets. No money. Sarah raced through the store, looking at the floor as she ran. She went down the milk aisle, the bread aisle, and finally to the aisle that had the beans. Still no money. She ran to the table that held the lettuce, looking carefully at the floor as she hurried from place to place. Still no money. What was she going to do? Her mother was never going to send her for groceries again.

She felt terrible. Suddenly, she noticed a darker color among the lettuce, and there it was. She was looking at the twenty-dollar bill. She must have dropped it when she looked at her list! Sarah felt the fear empty out of her body as she walked back to the counter to pay. The cashier smiled as she bagged the groceries. Sarah beamed back.

How to Teach

Plot is not easy to teach. In story writing, students usually encounter two major problems: They have trouble either distinguishing minor plot points from major ones or ordering the events in a natural sequence. Their stories begin to look like the *Family Circus* comic, in which a child goes around five houses to get to the other side of his yard. The goal is for students to understand which points are important and that plot contains a sequential rising action. To teach plot, you can use the model above and contrast it with the following poorly plotted model:

Sarah was going to the grocery store for her mother for the very first time. She had the grocery list and a twenty-dollar bill in her pocket. She went down the aisles and picked up a can of beans, lettuce, milk, and bread. She went to the cashier to pay and had lost her money! Sarah found the money in the lettuce. She happily paid for the groceries.

Compare the rising action in each model. Ask students, *Which story holds your interest and why? Which story lets you picture in your mind what is happening? Which story has more action? Which story is more exciting?* Visually mapping out the action on a plot line or listing the differences (as shown below) will help students make the comparison. Guide students to follow the sequence in the positive model and notice the lack of action in the negative model. Discuss how the author makes the action more exciting— how she makes it *rise*. For example, the well-written model has Sarah handing the cashier a piece of paper, which surprises the reader who assumes that Sarah is holding money.

Literature Sources for Other Models

Konigsburg, E. L. (1998). *The view from Saturday.* New York: Aladdin.

Raskin, E. (1978). *The Westing game.* New York: Dutton.

Poorly Plotted Model	**Well-Written Model**
Sarah goes to grocery store.	Sarah is excited. She is going to the grocery store by herself for the first time.
	Sarah feels like a grownup.
Sarah gets groceries.	Sarah gets the groceries.
Sarah tries to pay and has no money.	Sarah hands the cashier the money, but it isn't money. It's the grocery list.
	Sarah runs to look for the money.
	She looks all over the floor.
	She looks in the milk, bread, canned beans, and lettuce aisles.
Sarah finds the lost money in the lettuce.	Sarah finds the twenty dollars in the lettuce.
Sarah is happy.	Sarah and the cashier are both happy.

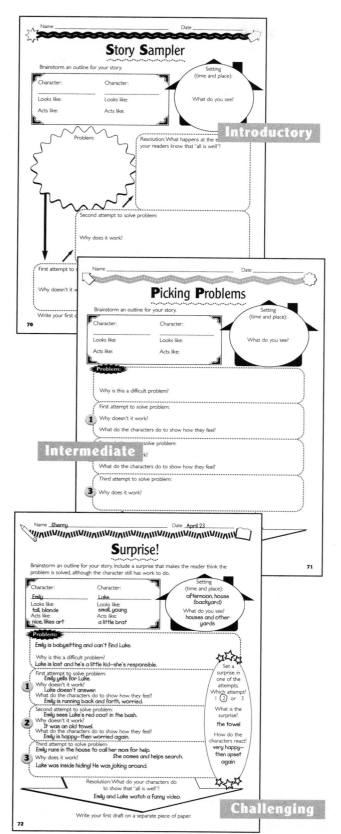

Fox, P. (1973). *The slave dancer.* New York: Bradbury Press.

Teacher to Teacher

When teaching plot, you may find it easier to start by having students write in pairs. Before writing the plot, students need to rehearse the story in their minds. Have them outline the plot on the graphic organizer, then go through the story by making a "movie in their mind." Ask, *Does it make sense? Does one event lead to the next? Is it exciting? Is there enough detail to make the story interesting?* Encourage them to revise their outline before they write the story.

Using the Tiered Organizers

When students understand that plot development includes not only a problem and solution, but also rising action, they are ready for one of the following graphic organizers.

Introductory: **Story Sampler**
Students write a story with one character and two sequential attempts to solve a problem.

Intermediate: **Picking Problems**
Students write a story with two characters and three sequential attempts to solve a problem. In addition, the character's feeling need to be implied.

Challenging: **Surprise!**
Students write a story as in Picking Problems and include a surprise—an addition of one or two sentences that makes the reader think there is no problem or that the problem has been solved when it actually has not.

Story **S**ampler

Brainstorm an outline for your story.

Character: _____

Looks like:

Acts like:

Character: _____

Looks like:

Acts like:

Setting
(time and place):

What do you see?

Problem:

Resolution: What happens at the end so
your readers know that "all is well"?

Second attempt to solve problem:

Why does it work?

First attempt to solve problem:

Why doesn't it work?

Write your first draft on a separate piece of paper.

Picking Problems

Brainstorm an outline for your story.

Character: _____

_____

Looks like:

Acts like:

Character: _____

_____

Looks like:

Acts like:

Setting
(time and place):

What do you see?

Problem:

Why is this a difficult problem?

1 First attempt to solve problem:

Why doesn't it work?

What do the characters do to show how they feel?

2 Second attempt to solve problem:

Why doesn't it work?

What do the characters do to show how they feel?

3 Third attempt to solve problem:

Why does it work?

Resolution: What do your characters do
to show that "all is well"?

Write your first draft on a separate piece of paper.

Surprise!

Brainstorm an outline for your story. Include a surprise that makes the reader think the problem is solved, although the character still has work to do.

Character: _____

Looks like:

Acts like:

Character: _____

Looks like:

Acts like:

Setting
(time and place):

What do you see?

Problem:

Why is this a difficult problem?

First attempt to solve problem:

1 Why doesn't it work?

What do the characters do to show how they feel?

Second attempt to solve problem:

2 Why doesn't it work?

What do the characters do to show how they feel?

Third attempt to solve problem:

3 Why does it work?

Set a surprise in one of the attempts. Which attempt? 1 2 or 3

What is the surprise?

How do the characters react?

Resolution: What do your characters do to show that "all is well"?

Write your first draft on a separate piece of paper.

Dialogue

Skill: *Develop realistic, purposeful dialogue.*

Overview

When used effectively, dialogue serves several important purposes. It can reveal relationships between characters, change the pace of the narrative, enhance the writer's voice, and provide information about the character, setting, problem, or solution. Compelling dialogue usually sounds realistic. It should be logical but not predictable. Most important, well-crafted dialogue contributes to the development of the story in some meaningful way. It should never just fill up space.

Model

> "Philip, Mr. Jacobs called about a half hour ago."
>
> "What did he want?"
>
> "He asked if you'd be interested in playing on his soccer team again this year. He needs a goalie."
>
> Philip stood still, staring at the phone on the wall for what seemed to be several minutes. He knew everyone would be disappointed when he told them he didn't want to play this year.
>
> "I'll call him tomorrow. He's probably eating dinner."
>
> "Eating dinner? It's only four o'clock. Call him. He's waiting for an answer."
>
> "I have to study for a history test. I'll do it later."

How to Teach

We want students to realize that strong dialogue holds the reader's attention because it sounds authentic. Common words—not words found in a thesaurus—are used.

Sometimes speakers are interrupted and never finish their thoughts. Other times, only phrases are used to convey ideas. Often, the speaker isn't identified, but the

reader knows who is speaking from what has been said.

As you read literature with students, point out examples of engaging dialogue, and discuss the impact of the dialogue in each story. Encourage students to identify an author whose dialogue most appeals to them. Building awareness of these features before beginning formal mini-lessons on dialogue helps prepare students for writing dialogue effectively.

In the model, the dialogue reveals Philip's reluctance to call Mr. Jacobs. Ask students why the writer used an incomplete sentence in the response "Eating dinner?" Help students see that it contributes to the authentic sound of the dialogue. Also have them consider why speakers' names are often left out of exchanges. In this case, can they infer who the second speaker is? Guide students to realize that the dialogue moves along faster this way. Use the following poorly written model to emphasize an ineffective approach to the same conversation.

"Hi, Mom," said Philip.

"Hi, Philip. How are you?" asked Mom.

"Good. How are you?" replied Philip.

"I'm okay. Mr. Jacobs telephoned. He called about a half an hour ago. He requested that you return his call," said Mom.

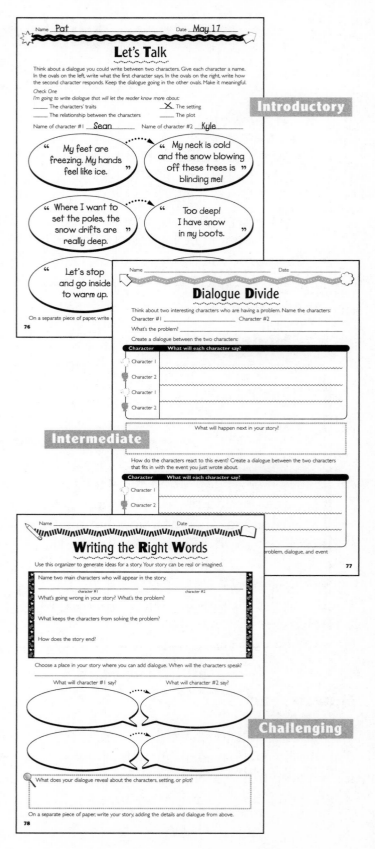

Let students contrast this version with the original to notice pacing, unnatural language, and unnecessary speaker cues. Next, prepare other examples of weak dialogue and ask students the following questions:

Does it sound authentic?

Does it move the story along?

Are there lines that could be eliminated or are all lines essential to the story?

What words or phrases could be changed to make it more effective?

Literature Sources for Other Models

Paterson, K. (1978). *The great Gilly Hopkins.* New York: The Trumpet Club. (The book begins with dialogue.)

Yolen, J. (1990). *The devil's arithmetic.* New York: Puffin Books. (The book begins with dialogue.)

Polacco, P. (2002). *When lightning comes in a jar.* New York: Philomel. (picture book)

Teacher to Teacher

Often when young writers attempt dialogue, it is stilted, predictable, and forced. In order to help students pay attention to how authentic dialogue sounds and move beyond tedious writing, have them listen in on conversations at the mall, during after-school activities, and on their way to and from school. Ask them to jot down exactly what is said in their writer's notebook or dialogue journal. By doing so, students will begin to focus on the vocabulary and rhythm of authentic dialogue.

Using the Tiered Organizers

When students understand the purpose of dialogue and can articulate the differences between effective and ineffective examples, they are ready to complete one of the following activities.

Introductory: **Let's Talk**
Students determine what they want a dialogue to reveal about characters, setting, or plot and then create a dialogue between two characters.

Intermediate: **Dialogue Divide**
Students use a conflict to create a dialogue between two characters, continue to move the story line by adding a plot point, and then change the pace by adding more dialogue.

Challenging: **Writing the Right Words**
Students plan out a story, decide where to include dialogue between two characters, and write it out. Then they provide a written response to the following prompt: What did your dialogue reveal about the characters, setting, or plot? Finally, they explain how the dialogue improved the quality of their writing.

Name _____ Date _____

Let's Talk

Think about a dialogue you could write between two characters. Give each character a name. In the ovals on the left, write what the first character says. In the ovals on the right, write how the second character responds. Keep the dialogue going in the other ovals. Make it meaningful.

Check One
I'm going to write dialogue that will let the reader know more about:

_____ The characters' traits   _____ The setting

_____ The relationship between the characters   _____ The plot

Name of character #1 _____   Name of character #2 _____

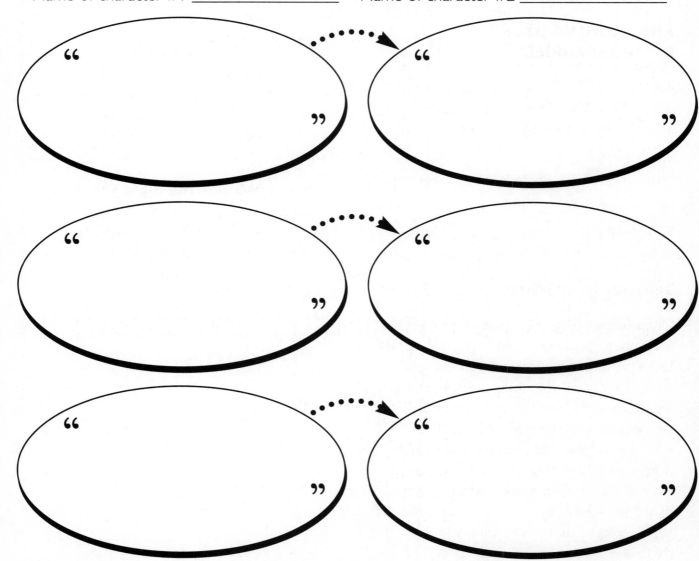

On a separate piece of paper, write out your dialogue.

Dialogue Divide

Think about two interesting characters who are having a problem. Name the characters:

Character #1 _____   Character #2 _____

What's the problem? _____

Create a dialogue between the two characters:

Character	What will each character say?
Character 1	〰〰〰〰〰〰〰〰〰〰〰〰〰〰〰〰〰〰
Character 2	
Character 1	〰〰〰〰〰〰〰〰〰〰〰〰〰〰〰〰〰〰
Character 2	

What will happen next in your story?

How do the characters react to this event? Create a dialogue between the two characters that fits in with the event you just wrote about.

Character	What will each character say?
Character 1	〰〰〰〰〰〰〰〰〰〰〰〰〰〰〰〰〰〰
Character 2	
Character 1	〰〰〰〰〰〰〰〰〰〰〰〰〰〰〰〰〰〰
Character 2	

On a separate piece of paper, write your story, adding the problem, dialogue, and event from above.

Writing the Right Words

Use this organizer to generate ideas for a story. Your story can be real or imagined.

Name two main characters who will appear in the story.

_____   _____
                character #1   character #2

What's going wrong in your story? What's the problem?

What keeps the characters from solving the problem?

How does the story end?

Choose a place in your story where you can add dialogue. When will the characters speak?

_____

What will character #1 say?   What will character #2 say?

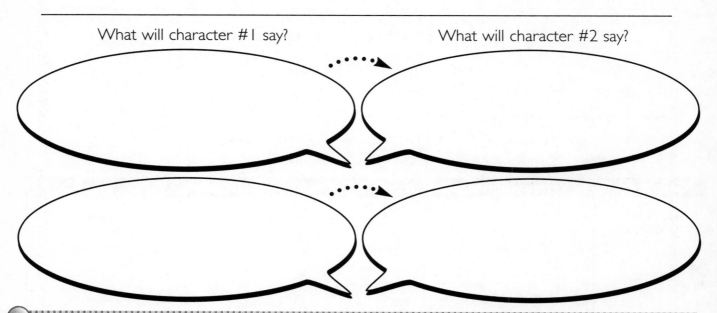

What does your dialogue reveal about the characters, setting, or plot?

On a separate piece of paper, write your story, adding the details and dialogue from above.

Memoir

Skill: *Write a story about a meaningful personal experience.*

Overview

We all have memories that we hold on to and replay. Some may be of good times; others may reflect sad or upsetting experiences. In either case, writing down these memories helps us learn about ourselves and about our relationships with others. This literary form invites writers to look back on something that really happened, not something wholly imagined. Memoirs may be about everyday events, but they are events that are worth remembering long after the events have passed. Written in the first person, memoirs contain a setting, a beginning, middle, and end. The author's feelings are clearly evident throughout.

Model

The Day I Hypnotized Mom

I was bored. I sat on the sofa eating popcorn and channel surfing. Finally, I settled on one of my favorite afternoon comedies. In this episode, a boy, who was about my age, was hypnotizing a man. I was fascinated by all the funny things the boy had the man do while he was hypnotized. At one point, he had the man pretend he was Elvis Presley. That's when I came up with my plan. "I bet I could do that," I whispered to myself.

I jumped up and raced to the dining room. I knew right where I could find some string and a spoon. I cut off an arm's length of string and tied it to the handle of the silver spoon. I was ready.

I walked into the kitchen, where my mom was preparing dinner. I asked Mom if she wanted to be hypnotized. Of course, my mom agreed.

I began to imagine all kinds of people and things I could make Mom become, but since I was new at this, I decided to make her into Elvis Presley. As I began to swing the string slowly in front of my mom's face, I chanted, "You are getting sleepy, you are getting very sleepy."

After the spoon swayed back and forth a few times, I told her that when I counted to three, she would begin to sing like Elvis. I counted, and right on cue, Mom began to sing "You Ain't Nothing but a Hound Dog." I was delighted. I could hardly believe that I was able to hypnotize Mom on my first try. This was soooo cool! Once the excitement started to dwindle, I decided that it was time to "unhypnotize" her. I couldn't wait to see Mom's reaction when I told her what I was able to do and what she had done.

I remembered exactly what the boy on TV did to unhypnotize the man, so I did the same thing. Looking straight into Mom's green eyes, I confidently announced, "When I clap my hands three times, you'll be back to your usual self." I clapped slowly and loudly as I counted the numbers, just as the boy on the TV show had done, but Mom continued to be Elvis, singing away as if nothing had happened. I began to panic. I didn't know what to do. It looked so easy on TV. I started to cry. Just then, my mother looked up from her make-believe guitar. When she saw how upset I was, she realized I didn't know she had only been pretending to be hypnotized. She bolted over and hugged me.

To this day, a good dozen years since I watched the man on TV get hypnotized, Mom and I still laugh about the day I hypnotized her.

How to Teach

Read aloud sections of several good memoirs. You may select some from those listed in the following section or use your own. Distribute copies of "The Day I Hypnotized Mom." Before reading the model aloud, give students these questions to think about while they listen:

> Do you know where this memoir takes place?
>
> Who is the main character?
>
> Why do you think the author wrote it?
>
> How is this memoir different from most stories?
>
> How is it similar to typical narratives?

After reading the memoir, have students form small groups to share answers to the questions. Next, gather together in a large group and record students' responses, comparing and contrasting narratives and memoirs in a Venn diagram. Guide students to articulate the elements of memoirs:

> A real-life, memorable event is recalled in enough detail to make it come alive for the reader.
>
> The setting is clearly identified.
>
> It has a strong beginning, middle, and end.
>
> It's written in first person; the word *I* is used often.
>
> There may be dialogue.
>
> Feelings are evident and unmistakable.

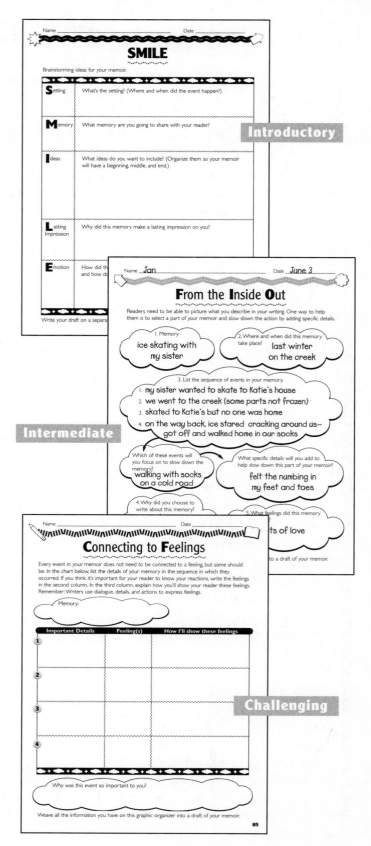

Distribute the sample SMILE graphic organizer. Review how the notes on the graphic organizer fit the criteria listed above.

Literature Sources for Other Models

Byars, B. (1991). *The moon and I*. Englewood Cliffs, NJ: J. Messner.

Yolen, J. (1987). *Owl moon*. New York: Philomel. (picture book)

Teacher to Teacher

You may want to model this form by sharing one of your own memories, thinking aloud as you plan what you will and will not include. Providing a rationale for your choices can reinforce the major elements you want students to include in their memoirs.

Using the Tiered Organizers

When students understand that memoirs are written to capture real-life events that have made lasting impressions, they are ready to complete one of the following activities.

Introductory: **SMILE (Setting, Memory, Ideas, Lasting Impression, Emotion)**
Students think about and organize the key elements of their memoir before composing a first draft.

Intermediate: **From the Inside Out**
Students think about and organize the key elements of their memoir before composing a first draft. In addition, they add relevant details in order to slow down the action.

Challenging: **Connecting to Feelings**
Students enrich their memoirs by connecting explicit feelings to some of the details and by explaining exactly how these feelings will be revealed to their readers.

SMILE

Brainstorming ideas for your memoir.

Setting : What's the setting? (Where and when did the event happen?)

In my kitchen when I was a young girl

Memory : What memory are you going to share with your reader?

When I hypnotized my mom

Ideas : What ideas do you want to include? (Organize them so your memoir will have a beginning, middle, and end.)

Watching a person get hypnotized on TV

Getting string and spoon   Getting scared

Hypnotizing mom   Getting a hug

Unhypnotizing her   Laughing now

Lasting Impression : Why did this memory make a lasting impression on you?

I was so scared at the time, but now I think it's funny that my mom played a trick on me when I was trying to play a trick on her.

Emotion : How did the event you described make you feel when it happened, and how does this memory make you feel now?

I was scared when it happened, but now I think it's funny.

Write your draft on a separate piece of paper.

SMILE

Brainstorming ideas for your memoir.

Setting	What's the setting? (Where and when did the event happen?)
Memory	What memory are you going to share with your reader?
Ideas	What ideas do you want to include? (Organize them so your memoir will have a beginning, middle, and end.)
Lasting Impression	Why did this memory make a lasting impression on you?
Emotion	How did the event you described make you feel when it happened, and how does this memory make you feel now?

Write your draft on a separate piece of paper.

From the Inside Out

Readers need to be able to picture what you describe in your writing. One way to help them is to select a part of your memoir and slow down the action by adding specific details.

1. Memory

2. Where and when did this memory take place?

3. List the sequence of events in your memory.

1.

2.

3.

4.

Which of these events will you focus on to slow down the memory?

What specific details will you add to help slow down this part of your memoir?

4. Why did you choose to write about this memory?

5. What feelings did this memory bring back?

Weave all the information you have on this graphic organizer into a draft of your memoir.

Connecting to Feelings

Every event in your memoir does not need to be connected to a feeling, but some should be. In the chart below, list the details of your memory in the sequence in which they occurred. If you think it's important for your reader to know your reactions, write the feelings in the second column. In the third column, explain how you'll show your reader these feelings. Remember: Writers use dialogue, details, and actions to express feelings.

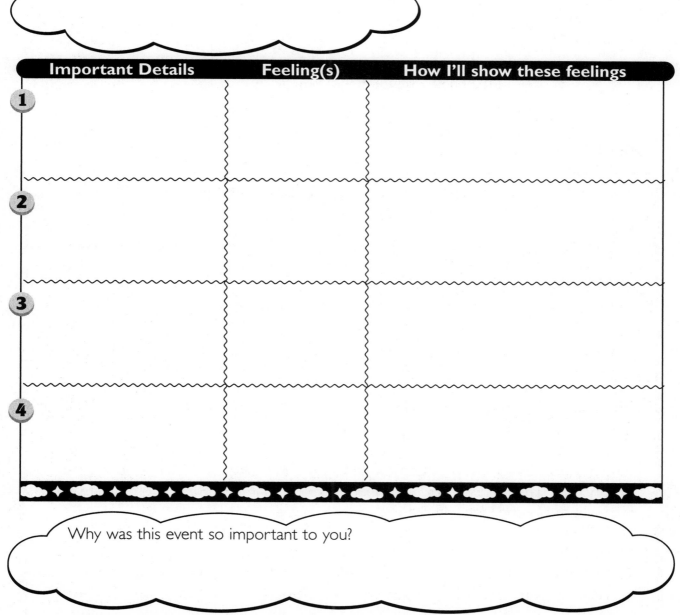

Memory:

	Important Details	Feeling(s)	How I'll show these feelings
1			
2			
3			
4			

Why was this event so important to you?

Weave all the information you have on this graphic organizer into a draft of your memoir.

Book Reports for Fiction

Skill: *Write a book report that includes a synopsis of the story and a recommendation for or against reading the book.*

Overview

Book report components vary from classroom to classroom, but two constants seem to be telling what the book is about (summarizing) and stating an opinion or giving a recommendation about the book. We have chosen the following criteria for book reports:

* book title
* author
* publisher
* publication date
* a synopsis of the book, excluding the ending
* recommendation for or against reading the book.

Model

Sing Down the Moon by Scott O'Dell
Houghton Mifflin Co., 1970

Sing Down the Moon by Scott O'Dell is a very powerful story about the problems of the Navaho nation in the 1860s. At that time, they were forced by the United States government to leave their homes and move to government-sanctioned areas.

Bright Morning, the main character, is a young girl who is "coming of age" in Navaho society, and soon it will be time for her to marry. She is interested in Tall Boy, but her parents think he is too proud and haughty. Bright Morning gets kidnapped by Spanish slavers, and sold into slavery. In a daring escape, with Tall Boy's much needed help, Bright Morning and another girl regain their freedom. Tall Boy's arm is terribly injured in the escape. Now Bright Morning's parents do not think that a man who can only use one arm is a good catch for their daughter.

Bright Morning's family members, along with all the Navajo people, are forced to leave their home in Canyon de Chelly and walk over 300 miles in what history calls "The Trail of Tears." The family is relocated in Fort Sumner, a desolate area where Navahos are without livelihood or hope.

How does Bright Morning cope? Scott O'Dell keeps us guessing to the end as Bright Morning and Tall Boy get themselves in and out of trouble. This book lets you see a sad part of our history and teaches us that we can survive the most horrible times in our life. I highly recommend this book.

How to Teach

By grade four, students usually have some experience with book reports and retellings. Discuss the components of a retelling: characters, setting, problem, attempts to solve, and solution. Students may have a rudimentary understanding of plot as the main problem, often with a number of smaller problems thrown in. These are important components in a book report. Explain that the writer of a book report has two purposes: to give readers a taste of what the book is about, and to persuade them to read or not to read a particular book.

When discussing book reports on fiction books, explain to students that they need to include the characters, the setting, the main problems, and some important points but not the solution, which would spoil it for other readers. Students who are able to distinguish between main and minor problems can add depth to their reports by including both types of problems. For example, in *Sing Down the Moon*, the main problem was the forced move of the Navajo people. A minor problem was the kidnapping of Bright Morning. Explain that in essence they are writing a summary of the book, without the ending. Their goal is to drum up interest so others will read the book.

(Please note that these ideas apply to reports on fiction. For nonfiction book reports, please refer to the summary writing chapter in our companion book, *Teaching Reading Through Differentiated Instruction With Leveled Graphic Organizers* by Witherell, N. and McMackin, M., Scholastic 2002/2005.)

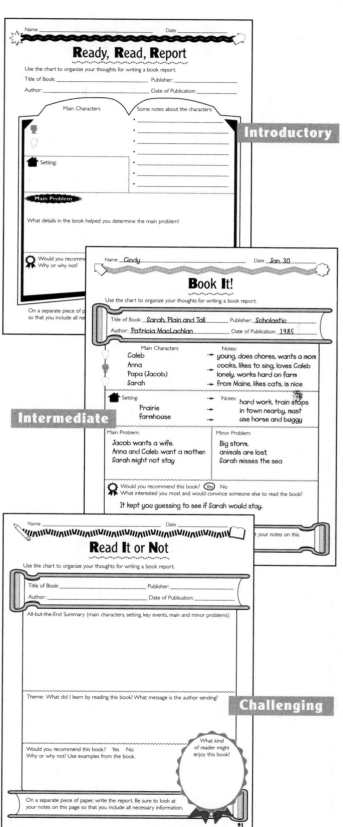

For the second purpose, persuading others to read or not read the book, point out that everyone has different tastes in reading, so although they may not have liked a book, someone else might. Recommendations need to be written in a way that sends this message. An opinion might read, "If you like to be scared, this is the book for you" or "After reading this book I know I don't want to climb Mount Everest, but it's a great book for people who think they may want to!"

Literature Sources for Other Models

For models of book reports, search the Web with the phrase "free elementary book reports." Make sure the model you find follows the same criteria that you would expect in your students' book reports.

Teacher to Teacher

In order to write effective reports on fiction books, students need to be familiar with story grammar: characters, setting, problem, attempts to solve, and solution. This will help them gather their thoughts to write organized book synopses. It may be beneficial to go over plot with the students as well (see pages 67–72).

Using the Tiered Organizers

When students are aware of the story elements and can identify important details, they are ready to complete one of the following graphic organizers.

Introductory: **Ready, Read, Report**
Students generate ideas for a book report, including main characters, setting, the problem, important details, and an opinion.

Intermediate: **Book It!**
Students generate ideas for a book report, including main characters, setting, the main problem, a minor problem, important details, and a persuasive opinion.

Challenging: **Read It or Not**
Students generate ideas for a book report, including main characters, setting, the main and minor problems with important details, the theme, and a persuasive opinion with support from the text.

Name _____   Date _____

Ready, **R**ead, **R**eport

Use the chart to organize your thoughts for writing a book report.

Title of Book: _____   Publisher: _____

Author: _____   Date of Publication: _____

Main Characters

Some notes about the characters:

• _____

• _____

• _____

• _____

Setting:

• _____

• _____

• _____

Main Problem

What details in the book helped you determine the main problem?

Would you recommend this book?   Yes   No
Why or why not?

On a separate piece of paper, write the report. Be sure to look at your notes on this page
so that you include all necessary information.

Book It!

Use the chart to organize your thoughts for writing a book report.

Title of Book: _____ Publisher: _____

Author: _____ Date of Publication: _____

Main Characters   →   Notes:

                                   →

                                   →

Setting: _____   →   Notes:

                                   →

                                   →

Main Problem: Minor Problem:

Would you recommend this book?   Yes   No
What interested you most and would convince someone else to read the book?

On a separate piece of paper, write the report. Be sure to look at your notes on this page so that you include all necessary information.

Name _____ Date _____

Read It or Not

Use the chart to organize your thoughts for writing a book report.

Title of Book: _____ Publisher: _____

Author: _____ Date of Publication: _____

All-but-the-End Summary (main characters, setting, key events, main and minor problems)

Theme: What did I learn by reading this book? What message is the author sending?

Would you recommend this book?   Yes   No
Why or why not? Use examples from the book.

What kind
of reader might
enjoy this book?

On a separate piece of paper, write the report. Be sure to look at
your notes on this page so that you include all necessary information.

Newspaper Article

Skill: *Write a newspaper article that opens with a lead, includes who, what, when, where, and why, and presents details in the body.*

Overview

Who, *what*, *where*, *when*, and *why* are the key words for gathering the information needed to write a newspaper article. In short articles, journalists are taught to write these ideas in the first paragraph, as the reader may stop there. The first few sentences are called the lead and answer most, if not all, of the "5 W's." This is where the reader expects to find the most significant news. The body of the story expands on the information in the lead, and the article ends with a neat conclusion.

Model

Dog Rescues Boy

by Rachel

Yesterday, in Buzzard's Bay, five-year-old Taylor Briggs went for an unexpected swim when rough seas threw him overboard. Taylor's dog, Biscuit, jumped overboard, grabbed Taylor by his life preserver, and brought him back to the boat. Taylor's dad, James Briggs, sailed the boat back to shore and praised the dog for a daring rescue.

Taylor was thrown off the boat late yesterday afternoon when the owner's craft was caught in a sudden storm, which caused the seas to get unusually high. Taylor, who was holding on to the edge of the boat, was washed overboard by an exceptionally high swell. Biscuit, hearing the boy scream, followed him into the water and swam after him. To the father's amazement, Biscuit clenched the boy's life-jacket cord between his teeth and pulled him to the boat.

According to Mr. Briggs, when Biscuit got Taylor near the boat, Taylor was able to grab on to the boat hook, and Briggs lifted him into the boat. Getting Biscuit back onboard proved to be a little tougher, but once Briggs got a rope around Biscuit's belly, he was able to lift the seventy-five pound dog into the boat.

In the words of Mr. Briggs, "That dog was saving my boy's life. No way could I leave him behind!" And what does Taylor say about his short swim? "The water was really, really cold!" It looked like Biscuit agreed as he wagged his tail and ate his treats.

How to Teach

Journalism is an exciting career. Journalists seem to always have the "inside scoop." That's what we want to convey when we write an article. To write effective articles, students need to know the criteria:

* The lead gives all the significant information: Who, What, When, Where, and Why (or How)

* The body gives more detailed information about what happened.

* The conclusion is interesting but does not contain important details.

Use the model to familiarize students with the text structure of a newspaper article. After students have read the entire article, point out that the 5 W's have been answered in the opening sentences, which comprise the lead. Help students to see that the second paragraph elaborates on this important information, giving the readers a clearer picture of what took place. Ask students if any of the 5 W's are in the final paragraph. (They are not.) Hold a short discussion on the interesting, yet unimportant details in the concluding paragraph. (Journalists are taught not to put important news in the conclusion; if there is not enough room in the paper, the ending paragraphs may be deleted.)

Next, hand out short articles from your local paper in which the criteria for a newspaper article are readily apparent. Working in partners, have students look at the first paragraph to see if they can answer the 5 W's. Instruct partners to

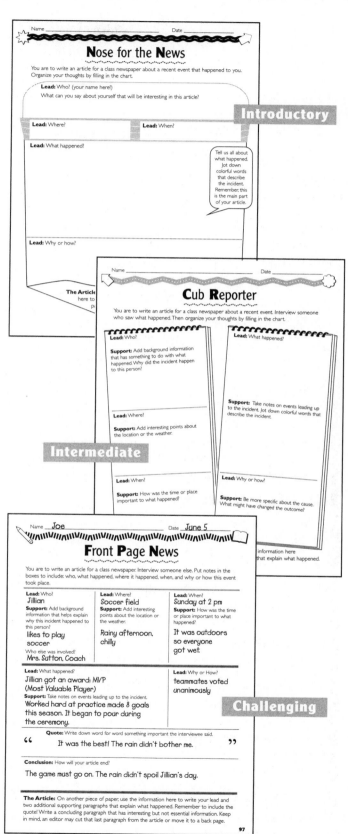

circle the first few sentences that make up the lead. After they have read the complete article, ask them to decide whether or not the concluding paragraph gives more important information. In most cases, it will not. Review the criteria for a newspaper article to make sure students clearly understand what belongs in the final product.

Journalists get the material for articles in different ways, including experiencing something personally, observing an event, interviewing someone, or through a combination of all three. Explain that one interviewing technique is to simply ask the 5 W's. A top journalist is able to get the person being interviewed to elaborate on the event, thereby acquiring interesting facts to include in the finished article. To keep the readers' interest, journalists often include a direct quote from the person being interviewed.

Literature Sources for Other Models

Any local newspaper.

Kids' Week, Time for Kids, Scholastic News, Weekly Reader (any newspaper written for classrooms).

Web newspaper articles such as those found at *Sports Illustrated for Kids* (www.sikids.com) and Kids' Newsroom (Kidsnewsroom.org).

Teacher to Teacher

Students should be familiar with newspaper articles before they start to write their own. If newspaper articles are used for tracking current events or another instructional purpose in your classroom, have students start to identify the 5 W's in the articles. Being aware of the way published articles are structured will give students a framework for writing their own articles.

Using the Tiered Organizers

Once your students can circle the lead of a paragraph and identify the 5 W's, they are ready for one of the following tiered activities.

Introductory: **Nose for the News**
Students generate ideas for a newspaper article on something that happened to them, including the 5 W's, and then write a lead and one supporting paragraph that includes this information.

Intermediate: **Cub Reporter**
Students interview a partner and generate ideas for a newspaper article, including the 5 W's, and then write a lead that includes this information. They write two supporting paragraphs that offer more details about the incident.

Challenging: **Front Page News**
Students will interview a partner and generate ideas for a newspaper article including who, what, where, when, and why or how, and write a lead that includes this information. The article will include three supporting paragraphs that expand on the information found in the lead, supported by at least one quote. They will also write a concluding paragraph, which contains interesting but unimportant details.

Nose for the News

You are to write an article for a class newspaper about a recent event that happened to you. Organize your thoughts by filling in the chart.

Lead: Who? (your name here!)

What can you say about yourself that will be interesting in this article?

Lead: Where?

Lead: When?

Lead: What happened?

> Tell us all about what happened. Jot down colorful words that describe the incident. Remember, this is the main part of your article.

Lead: Why or how?

The Article: On another piece of paper, use the information here to write your lead and at least one supporting paragraph that explains what happened.

Cub Reporter

You are to write an article for a class newspaper about a recent event. Interview someone who saw what happened. Then organize your thoughts by filling in the chart.

Lead: Who?

Support: Add background information that has something to do with what happened. Why did the incident happen to this person?

Lead: Where?

Support: Add interesting points about the location or the weather.

Lead: When?

Support: How was the time or place important to what happened?

Lead: What happened?

Support: Take notes on events leading up to the incident. Jot down colorful words that describe the incident.

Lead: Why or how?

Support: Be more specific about the cause. What might have changed the outcome?

The Article: On another piece of paper, use the information here to write your lead and two additional supporting paragraphs that explain what happened.

Front Page News

You are to write an article for a class newspaper. Interview someone else. Put notes in the boxes to include: who, what happened, where it happened, when, and why or how this event took place.

Lead: Who?

Support: Add background information that helps explain why this incident happened to this person?

Who else was involved?

Lead: Where?

Support: Add interesting points about the location or the weather.

Lead: When?

Support: How was the time or place important to what happened?

Lead: What happened?

Support: Take notes on events leading up to the incident.

Lead: Why or How?

Quote: Write down word for word something important the interviewee said.

" "

Conclusion: How will your article end?

The Article: On another piece of paper, use the information here to write your lead and two additional supporting paragraphs that explain what happened. Remember to include the quote! Write a concluding paragraph that has interesting but not essential information. Keep in mind, an editor may cut that last paragraph from the article or move it to a back page.

Friendly and Business Letters

Skill: *Write meaningful messages and use the correct formats for friendly and business letters.*

Overview

Friendly letters are written to close friends who usually share common experiences and a knowledge of the same topics. In such cases, writers do not need to include a wealth of details. The reader is able to draw on the common knowledge and experiences to fill in the gaps and construct meaning. On the other hand, business letters are usually written to unknown readers who may not share the writer's knowledge and experiences. The more distant the relationship between reader and writer, the more explicit the writing needs to be (Kaufer, D. S., & Carley, K., 1994).

Model

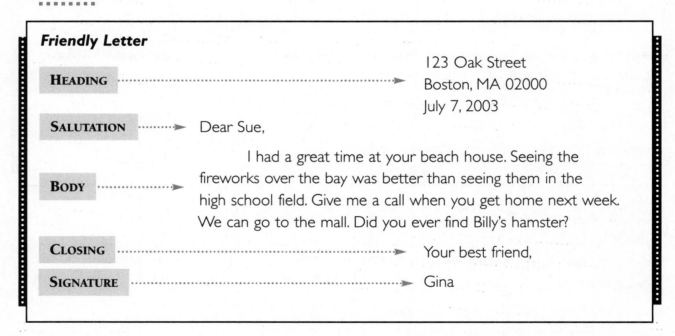

Friendly Letter

HEADING — 123 Oak Street
Boston, MA 02000
July 7, 2003

SALUTATION — Dear Sue,

BODY — I had a great time at your beach house. Seeing the fireworks over the bay was better than seeing them in the high school field. Give me a call when you get home next week. We can go to the mall. Did you ever find Billy's hamster?

CLOSING — Your best friend,

SIGNATURE — Gina

How to Teach

There are two important components of letter writing: purpose, which is to communicate ideas, and format.

Friendly Letters:

It's fun to begin work on letter writing with an exercise that helps students realize that communicating ideas has a great deal to do with the relationship the writer has with the reader. Explain to students that when both parties share a great deal in common, the writing can be less detailed and specific than when the recipient doesn't share the same experiences and knowledge. To make this point, ask students to tell about a common

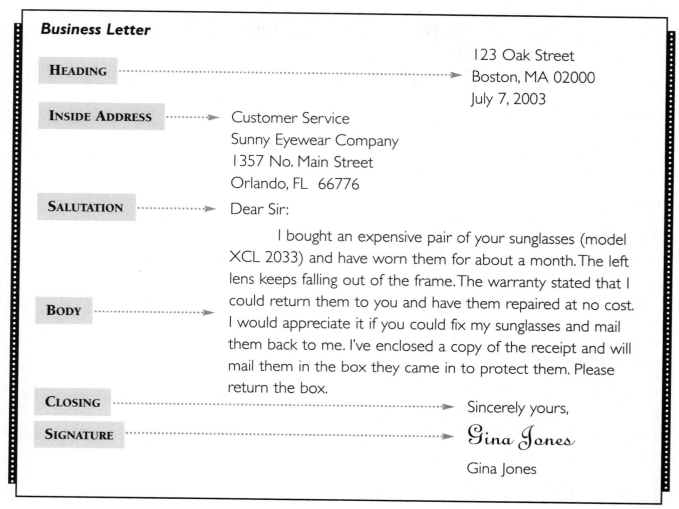

Business Letter

HEADING ··· ➤ 123 Oak Street
Boston, MA 02000
July 7, 2003

INSIDE ADDRESS ·········· ➤ Customer Service
Sunny Eyewear Company
1357 No. Main Street
Orlando, FL 66776

SALUTATION ················· ➤ Dear Sir:

BODY ················· ➤   I bought an expensive pair of your sunglasses (model XCL 2033) and have worn them for about a month. The left lens keeps falling out of the frame. The warranty stated that I could return them to you and have them repaired at no cost. I would appreciate it if you could fix my sunglasses and mail them back to me. I've enclosed a copy of the receipt and will mail them in the box they came in to protect them. Please return the box.

CLOSING ···································· ➤ Sincerely yours,

SIGNATURE ······························· ➤ *Gina Jones*

Gina Jones

experience, such as how they got to school that day. A typical response would be:

    Joel and Steve: *We got a ride from Tom's mom.*

Record their answers. Make sure students notice what information is given and what information is assumed. For example, Joel and Steve assume everyone knows who Tom is, where all of them live, and maybe even what type of car or truck Tom's mom drives.

    Segue from this exercise to the model **friendly letter**. Have students apply what they just learned: Gina and Sue share common experiences and knowledge, so Gina doesn't have to explain about the fireworks at the high school, give details about which mall they'll visit, or provide information about Billy or what happened to his hamster. Gina's tone is friendly and her ideas are clear enough for Sue to understand.

    Next, consider the format (see the template on page 105). Point out where lines are skipped and commas are used. A colleague of ours glues elbow macaroni on the chart to represent commas—having this 3-D reminder can be helpful and fun. Finally, explain that we capitalize only the first word in the closing.

Business Letters:

On another day, take a close look at Gina's business letter. Now Gina is writing to someone she has never met, who lives far away, and who has not experienced what Gina has experienced. To convey her message, Gina must clearly explain the purpose for her letter (to have her sunglasses repaired), include specific details (model number, warranty information, a copy of the receipt, and what she wants the recipient to do), and express her ideas in a logical order (purpose for the letter, rationale for returning the glasses, her expectations). Next, consider the format (see the template for a business letter, page 106). Point out where lines are skipped and where punctuation is used.

Comparing and Contrasting Friendly and Business Letters:

Display a friendly letter and a business letter on chart paper. With different colored markers, highlight differences in the parts of each letter, the number of lines skipped between parts of each letter, and the punctuation.

Literature Sources for Other Models

Hesse, K. (1992). *Letters from Rifka.* New York: Henry Holt and Company.

Stewart, S. (1997). *The gardener.* New York: Farrar, Straus & Giroux. (picture book)

Teague, M. (2002). *Dear Mrs. LaRue: Letters from obedience school.* New York: Scholastic. (picture book)

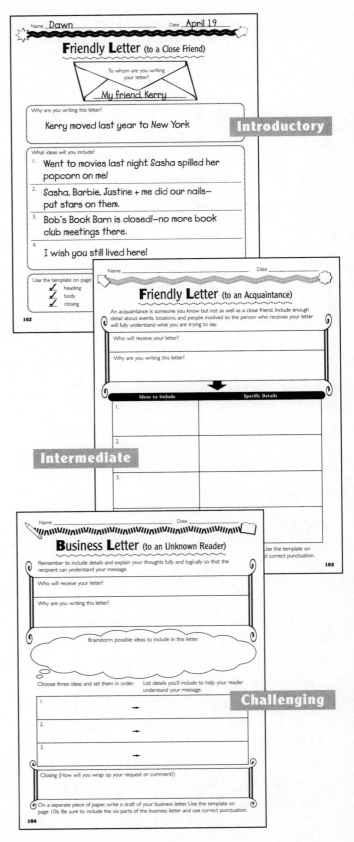

Teacher to Teacher

It is developmentally appropriate to have less accomplished writers create letters for people they already know. Through the process, they learn that writing is a form of communication. Gradually, however, it is important for students to learn how to write to people who do not share common experiences. As they progress through school and beyond, more of their writing will be to people beyond their immediate proximity.

Using the Tiered Organizers

As you work with students on format, also look to see which ones understand the requirements of communicating with someone who is separated by location, time, knowledge, and experiences. Ask these students to share their letters and explain what they did to ensure that their messages would be clearly understood.

Introductory: **A Friendly Letter (to a Close Friend)**

Students record whom the letter is for, the purpose of the letter, and ideas to include in the letter. They write a friendly letter, using the template on page 105 as a guide.

Intermediate: **A Friendly Letter (to an Acquaintance)**

Students record whom the letter is for, the purpose of the letter, and ideas to include in the letter. Because they are writing for a less familiar reader, students specify explicit details to help bridge the gap in time, location, knowledge, and experiences between writer and reader. They write a friendly letter, using the template on page 105 as a guide.

Challenging: **A Business Letter (to an Unknown Reader)**

Students determine an appropriate audience (person or business) and purpose for a letter, such as to request information or assistance, express satisfaction or dissatisfaction about a product, let a political leader know what they think about important issues. Using the template on page 106 as a guide, they draft a business letter that includes relevant details and a closing.

Friendly **L**etter (to a Close Friend)

To whom are you writing
your letter?

_____

Why are you writing this letter?

What ideas will you include?

1.

_____

2.

_____

3.

_____

4.

On a separate sheet of paper, write your letter. Check to make sure you include a

____ heading   ____ signature

____ body   ____ comma after the salutation

____ closing   ____ comma after the closing

Friendly Letter (to an Acquaintance)

An acquaintance is someone you know but not as well as a close friend. Include enough detail about events, locations, and people involved so the person who receives your letter will fully understand what you are trying to say.

Who will receive your letter?

Why are you writing this letter?

Ideas to Include	Specific Details
1.	
2.	
3.	
4.	

On a separate sheet of paper, write a draft of your friendly letter. Be sure to include the five parts of the friendly letter and correct punctuation.

Business Letter (to an Unknown Reader)

Remember to include details and explain your thoughts fully and logically so that the recipient can understand your message.

Who will receive your letter?

Why are you writing this letter?

Brainstorm possible ideas to include in this letter.

Choose three ideas and set them in order.   List details you'll include to help your reader understand your message.

1.	→
2.	→
3.	→

Closing (How will you wrap up your request or comment?)

On a separate piece of paper, write a draft of your business letter. Be sure to include the six parts of the business letter and use correct punctuation.

Format for a Friendly Letter

_____

_____ Heading

_____

Skip 2 lines

Salutation _____ ,

Skip 1 line

Body
_____

_____

_____

_____

_____

_____

_____

_____

_____

_____

_____

Skip 2 lines

Closing _____ ,

Signature _____

Format for a **B**usiness **L**etter

_____

_____ Heading

_____

Skip 4 lines

_____

Inside   _____

Address   _____

                _____

Skip 2 lines

Salutation   _____(:)_____

Skip 2 lines

                _____

                _____

                _____

Body   _____

                _____

                _____

                _____

Skip 2 lines

Closing   _____(,)___

Skip 4 lines

Signature   _____

Writing to Prompts on High-Stake Tests

Skill: *Write a well-structured, detailed response to a prompt.*

Overview

Students across the country are being asked to demonstrate their writing skills on high-stake tests. It's becoming increasingly important for them to be able to provide clear, focused, detailed responses to prompts. Writing to a prompt involves several interrelated components: topic and idea development, organization of ideas, sentence structure, word choice, and conventions. Before beginning this chapter, find out what your students will be tested on, and review related chapters in this book (narrative, compare-contrast, persuasive). In this chapter, we focus on the reading-writing connection as students move from prompt to draft.

Model

Prompt: Most people have a favorite month. Tell which month is your favorite and explain why it is your favorite month.

July is my favorite month. There are many reasons why I like July. First, I like it because it begins with a holiday, July 4th. Every year, our town sets off fireworks on July 3rd. This year I was old enough to watch them with my friends instead of my family. The fireworks lasted for about 30 minutes. There were several new ones this year, including a set of red, white, and blue fireworks that <u>went off</u> while <u>everyone</u> sang "the bombs bursting in air" during the National Anthem. The whole sky lit up at the end when they set off lots of fireworks <u>at the same time</u>. I bet you could see and hear them for miles around. On the 4th, there is a big parade that goes right near my house. There are fire engines, bands, clowns, floats, and antique cars in the parade. Men and women sell big balloons and noisemakers along the parade route. When the parade is over, I feel like m-a-r-c-h-i-n-g back to my house, even on those <u>hot</u> July days. In fact, I like it hot in July, especially when I can go to Nelson Lake. I can swim out to one of the two rafts and <u>jump</u> off. If my friends are there, we have races between the rafts. As you can see, July is my favorite month for lots of good reasons.

How to Teach

The key components of successful writing on standardized tests are:

(1) Understanding direction words: We've found that some students falter on their responses simply because they don't know what the direction word is asking them to do. Take a few minutes to reinforce this vocabulary: *compare, contrast, describe, persuade, explain, list,* and so on. Distribute a list of common direction words and their definitions for students to keep in their writing folders.

(2) Reading actively: Using the prompt and colored pencils, have students circle important words (such as direction words) and number the pieces of the prompt that require a response. In the prompt above, *favorite* and *month* are important for understanding what is expected. They should be circled.

(3) Writing the topic sentence: Show students that the prompt was reworded to create the topic sentence. Underline words in the prompt that were used in the response.

(4) Adding details: Next, ask, *What details were included in the model response and how did the writer elaborate on each one so you can see exactly what is being described?* On a two-column chart with the headings *details* and *elaborations-descriptions,* record answers and talk about how the details were used to fully answer the prompt.

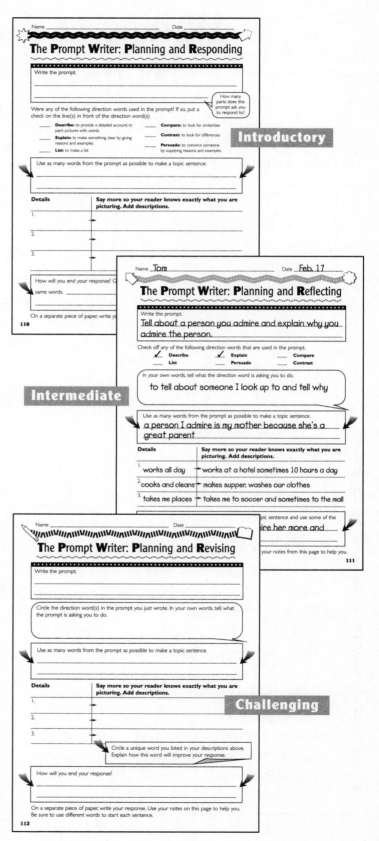

(5) Making the writing sound magnificent (we could have said *good* but chose not to):

Sentence structure: Students need to know how to vary sentence beginnings (moving away from *Then… and then…*). To drive this point home, try this exercise, which we learned from a wonderful fifth grade teacher. Have students circle the words at the beginning of each sentence and count up how many times each word is repeated. Follow this exercise by sharing many samples of varied sentence beginnings. Remind students that sentence beginnings shouldn't "echo" through the essay.

Word choice: Finally, focus on a few words and phrases in the model that are not unique or specific, such as "went off," "everyone," "at the same time," "hot," and "jump." Divide students into teams and have them find as many synonyms as they can to use in place of these words. The replacements must maintain the meaning of the original words, but they should be more specific, creative, precise, or novel. Encourage everyone to use a thesaurus and hunt for magnificent words.

Teacher to Teacher

As students become confident and skilled writers, you'll want to move them beyond simply rewording the prompt to make the topic sentence. More accomplished writers use strategies that invite the reader into the piece in interesting ways, such as beginning with an engaging open-ended question. Finally, encourage students to write clearly and go beyond a cursory response to the prompt. Many times, students miss points because they fail to answer the prompt fully or write legibly.

Using the Tiered Organizers

The graphic organizers are designed to introduce a structure for writing responses to high-stake prompts. When students understand the process involved in writing an effective response, they are ready to be matched to one of the leveled activities.

Introductory: **The Prompt Writer: Planning and Responding**
Students determine the direction word(s) in the prompt, identify the steps required to answer the prompt, change the prompt to a topic sentence, provide details and elaborate on them, and write a conclusion to the response.

Intermediate: **The Prompt Writer: Planning and Reflecting**
Students complete all the activities in the introductory organizer, and they are expected to know the meaning of the direction words and be able to define them—no definitions are provided.

Challenging: **The Prompt Writer: Planning and Revising**
Students complete all the activities in the intermediate organizer. In addition, they select a unique word from their descriptions and explain how it improves their response to the prompt. Finally, they use different words to start each sentence.

The Prompt Writer: Planning and Responding

★ ★

Write the prompt.

_____

_____

> How many parts does this prompt ask you to respond to?

Were any of the following direction words used in the prompt? If so, put a check on the line(s) in front of the direction word(s)

_____ **Describe:** to provide a detailed account; to paint pictures with words

_____ **Explain:** to make something clear by giving reasons and examples

_____ **List:** to make a list

_____ **Compare:** to look for similarities

_____ **Contrast:** to look for differences

_____ **Persuade:** to convince someone by supplying reasons and examples

Use as many words from the prompt as possible to make a topic sentence.

_____

_____

Details	Say more so your reader knows exactly what you are picturing. Add descriptions.
1.	
2.	
3.	

How will you end your response? Go back to your topic sentence and use some of the same words. _____

_____

On a separate piece of paper, write your response. Use your notes from this page to help you.

The **P**rompt **W**riter: **P**lanning and **R**eflecting

★ ★

Write the prompt.

_____

_____

In your own words, tell what the direction word is asking you to do.

Use as many words from the prompt as possible to make a topic sentence.

_____

_____

Details	Say more so your reader knows exactly what you are picturing. Add descriptions.
1.	_____
2.	_____
3.	_____

How will you end your response? Go back to your topic sentence and use some of the

same words. _____

_____

On a separate piece of paper, write your response. Use your notes from this page to help you.

The Prompt Writer: Planning and Revising

★★

Write the prompt.

_____

_____

Circle the direction word(s) in the prompt you just wrote. In your own words, tell what the prompt is asking you to do.

Use as many words from the prompt as possible to make a topic sentence.

_____

_____

Details	**Say more so your reader knows exactly what you are picturing. Add descriptions.**
1.	_____
2.	_____
3.	_____

Circle a unique word you listed in your descriptions above. Explain how this word will improve your response.

How will you end your response?

_____

_____

On a separate piece of paper, write your response. Use your notes on this page to help you. Be sure to use different words to start each sentence.